Printing and Publishing Terms

Martin H. Manser

Chambers Commercial Reference

© W & R Chambers Ltd Edinburgh, 1988

Published by W & R Chambers Ltd Edinburgh, 1988

British Library Cataloguing in Publication Data
Manser, Martin H.
    Printing and publishing terms.—(Chambers commercial reference
    series).
    1. Printing—Dictionaries 2. Publishers and publishing
    —Dictionaries
    I. Title
    070.5'03'21   Z118
ISBN 0-550-18067-2

Printed in Great Britain by Richard Clay Ltd, Bungay, Suffolk

Preface

Printing and Publishing Terms is a compact but comprehensive reference book which has been specially written to meet the needs of school and college students on a wide range of business and vocational courses at intermediate level.

Along with the other titles in the Chambers Commercial Reference series, *Printing and Publishing Terms* provides up-to-date explanations of the key terms used in various areas of business activity. All words and abbreviations are listed alphabetically and defined in clear simple English.

Although intended as a companion to course studies, *Printing and Publishing Terms* is also an ideal reference text for those already working in a commercial environment. The book will prove to be an invaluable companion to their work.

Printing and Publishing Terms

Martin H. Manser is an experienced reference-book editor who has compiled a wide range of reference books and dictionaries.

Aa

A series; A sizes A system of trimmed metric paper sizes. In every size within the A series, the proportion of the short side to the long side remains the same, $1:\sqrt{2}$. This offers advantages for enlargements and reductions. See **paper sizes**.

AAs (*US*) Abbreviation of *author's alterations*; see **author's corrections.**

abridged edition The shortened version of a book.

abstract A very short version of a book or article, which summarises the main points.

accent A mark or symbol used to show the pronunciation of a letter in a particular language. The most common include acute as in é, cedilla as in ç, circumflex as in ê, grave as in è, tilde as in ñ, umlaut as in ü.

accordion fold (*US*) See **concertina fold.**

acetate See **cellulose acetate.**

acknowledgments The part of the preliminary pages of a book in which the author or editor thanks those who assisted in the preparation and publication of the book. The sources of all quotations, illustrations, etc., may also be listed in the acknowledgments.

acoustic coupler A device which converts electrical pulses by a modem to sound (acoustic waves) for transmission and reception along telephone lines to and from a computer, permitting computers to be connected along these lines with a terminal by a modem and telephone handset. The device is not wired into the telephone system; the connection is made by a small microphone and loudspeaker that are positioned close to the earpiece and mouthpiece of an ordinary telephone handset.

ACs Abbreviation of **author's corrections.**

acute The accent ´. See also **accent.**

addendum (plural *addenda*) Supplementary material in a book. It is printed at the beginning or end of the main text.

additive primaries The colours red, green, and blue. When combined, these colours produce white light.

additive process A photographic process in which the colours that are wanted are produced by mixing the primary colours red, green, and blue.

adhesive binding See **perfect binding.**

advance A sum of money paid by a publisher to an author in advance of publication of a book. The advance is set against subsequent royalty payments.

advanced copy; **advance** One of a limited quantity of finished copies of a new book, delivered by the printer to the publisher before delivery of the main bulk order. Advanced copies are used especially for promotional purposes.

against the grain Folding or marking paper or feeding paper to a printing press at right angles to the direction of the grain of the paper.

agate (*US*) See **ruby.**

agate line (*US*) A measure of the depth of advertising space, equal to one column wide and one-fourteenth of an inch deep.

agent (1) A person or organisation that acts and negotiates on behalf of an author or publisher for the sale of rights in literary works. Agents take a percentage of money received for their services. Also known as **literary agent.** (2) An organisation that holds stocks of books for various publishers in a foreign country, for sale to book-sellers in that country.

air   An amount of space on a printed page that contains no printed matter.

airbrush   A device that sprays paint or ink by means of compressed air. The instrument reduces the liquid to a fine spray that is ejected through a nozzle. It is used in illustrations to obtain tone effects and when retouching photographs.

album paper   A type of antique paper made of wood pulp, used especially for the pages of photograph albums.

alignment   The arrangement of type and other graphic matter to be perfectly level in one horizontal or vertical line.

all edges gilt   Describing a book having the top, side, and bottom trimmed edges of the pages coloured gold. Also *aeg*.

all up   Used to describe the completion of all the setting of the text.

alphabet length   The length of the lower-case letters of the alphabet in a particular fount.

alphanumeric   An acronym formed from the words *alpha*betic and *numeric*. Alphanumeric refers to those keys on a keyboard that represent letters and numbers rather than symbols and special functions. An alphanumeric keyboard is one similar to that on a typewriter or computer. An alphanumeric set is a complete set of letters and numbers, sometimes also including punctuation marks and other symbols.

alterations   The changes made to the main text of a book after it has been proofread.

American standard code for information interchange
An international standard computer code in which eight

binary bits are combined to represent letters, numbers, and symbols on a computer keyboard. Most VDUs and printers use this code. Also *ASCII*.

ampersand   The character & meaning 'and'.

angle brackets   The signs < > used in literary texts, scientific and mathematical works, etc.

annex   (chiefly *US*) A supplementary part to the main text of a book.

annotate   To provide additional comments or explanations (annotations) to a text.

anodised plate   (In offset printing) a plate coated with a hardened film so that it will be protected from wearing down.

anthology   A collection of literary passages, especially poetry, written by various authors and selected by a compiler or editor.

antiquarian   (Of books) old and rare, sometimes used to describe books that are over 75 years old and unavailable from the publisher.

antique   A type of book paper that is not calendered or coated. Antique paper has a rough finish and is light and moderately bulky.

appendix   (plural   *appendices*)   Additional   material supplementary to the main text, and printed at the end of a book.

approval copy   A copy of a book sent to a lecturer, teacher, etc., for his or her recommendation to students. The copy must be returned or paid for, or may be retained free of charge if a certain number of additional copies of the book are ordered.

apron   (*US*) Additional space allowed at the margins of a page for a fold-out.

Arabic numerals   The numbers 1 2 3 4 5 6 7 8 9 0 . Contrast with *Roman numerals*.

arrow-head   The symbol shaped like the striking end of an arrow, used for example to introduce a cross-reference.

art   (*US*) Abbreviation of **artwork.**

art paper   Paper coated with a composition containing china clay, used for printing illustrations, especially fine-screen (i.e. 150 lines per inch) half-tones. It has a hard smooth surface.

artwork   Illustrations and other decorative material—especially material other than text only—prepared and arranged for reproduction.

ascender   The part of a lower-case letter that extends above the top of the letter *x*, for example *d*, *h*. Contrast with *descender*.

ASCII   See **American standard code for information interchange.**

ASPIC   Authors' Symbolic Pre-press Interfacing Codes; a set of codes used to signify the typographical in-structions of a computer or word processor to typesetting equipment.

asterisk   The sign * used as a (first-level) reference mark, especially to a footnote.

auction   In publishing, a method of selling books and rights by inviting bids. The person making the highest bid becomes the buyer.

author   The writer, compiler, or editor of a book, article, etc., for example when considered as one party of an agreement with a publisher for a literary work.

author questionnaire   A form that an author fills out for a publisher on the likely markets for the book, competi-tive titles, etc. The answers are useful in the marketing of the book.

author tour   A tour made by an author to several diffe-rent locations, to help promote his or her book. An author tour may include visits to bookshops or colleges to sell and sign copies of the book and interviews on radio or television programmes.

author's copies (Usually six) complimentary copies of a book that a publisher gives to the author on publication of his or her book.

author's corrections Corrections that an author makes to galley proofs that alter the original text. The typesetter charges for the cost of making such corrections, while no charge is made for correcting the typesetter's errors. Also *ACs*. US equivalent: *author's alterations* (*AAs*).

author's proofs The set of galley proofs that are sent to an author for further checking. This set has sometimes already been read by the typesetter and corrected against the original manuscript.

auto indent An instruction to a computerised typesetting machine to indent the output text automatically.

autobiography The description of a person's life written by that person.

automatic dictionary The part of a computer or word processor that automatically checks the spelling of the text that has been keyed in.

automatic page make-up The automatic arrangement of typeset material onto a page. Details of the size of the page such as the number of lines, instructions on the location of headings and page numbers are inserted into the computer and the make-up is produced automatically without being checked on a visual display unit.

a/w Abbreviation of **artwork.**

Bb

B Abbreviation of **binding.** See **BDG.**

B series; B sizes A series of untrimmed metric paper sizes for posters, wall charts, etc. The B series is used when the difference in size between sheets in the A series is too great. The sizes are:

B0	1000 mm ×	1414 mm
B1	707 mm ×	1000 mm
B2	500 mm ×	707 mm
B3	353 mm ×	500 mm
B4	250 mm ×	353 mm
B5	176 mm ×	250 mm
B6	125 mm ×	176 mm
B7	88 mm ×	125 mm
B8	62 mm ×	88 mm
B9	44 mm ×	62 mm
B10	31 mm ×	44 mm

back-jacket flap The part of the printed paper cover on a hardback book that folds inside the back cover.

back lining A strip of paper or fabric, e.g. linen or gauze, that is glued to the spine of a hardcover book to strengthen the joint when the case is applied.

back margin (or **back**) The margin of a book that is nearest the edge at which pages are bound.

back matter (*US*) See **endmatter.**

back-up copy A copy made of the working disk sometimes done daily or weekly in the event of accident to the working disk so that all data is not lost completely. The back-up copy disks are normally stored in a separate area to the working disks.

backbone   The back bound edge of a book. See **spine**.

background   The part of an image in a photograph or illustration that appears furthest from the viewer.

backing-up   Printing on the second side of a sheet of paper when the first side has already been printed. Also known as **back to back; perfecting.**

backlist   The books which a publisher has published before the current season that are still available.

backslant   A typeface that slopes backwards. Such slanting to the left can be obtained electronically in phototypesetting.

bad break   An unsightly division of the text, for example starting a page, especially a left-hand page, with a hyphenated word or ending a paragraph with a word at the top of a page or column.

balance   The harmonious integration of different elements of a layout or design, for example between text and line drawings on facing pages.

balloon   An approximately circular figure enclosing the words or thoughts of a character in a cartoon.

banda   A spirit duplicator for which a master must be prepared by writing or typing on master paper with a sheet of hectographic carbon paper placed against the glossy side of the paper. A reversed image is obtained on the back of the master paper and the prepared master is fixed to the drum of the banda (or duplicator) so that as the sheets of duplicating paper are fed through, they are damped by a fluid which activates the dye on the master. The image is then transferred the correct way round onto the duplicating paper.

bank paper   A thin uncoated paper, in a range of 45 gm² to 63 gm² weights, used for carbon copies, airmail letters, etc.

banner   A headline in large type extending across the full width of a newspaper page. Also known as **banner headline.**

bar code   A printed machine-readable code in the form of vertical lines used on packaging and book covers to identify and contain information about a product. Bar codes can be read by a wand, light pen, or bar-code scanner. An application is in the labelling of retail products where the wand is used to record the sale at the time and place of purchase and to control stock. The two most frequently used types are the EAN (European Article Number) and the American UPC (Universal Product Code).

base   The metal or wooden block on which the printing plate is mounted in letterpress printing, to bring it up to the height of the type.

base alignment   In phototypesetting, the arrangement of type of different typefaces and sizes to be level with an imaginary line connecting the foot of capital letters.

base artwork   The bottommost set of artwork that requires the addition of overlays, as to show different colours.

base line   The imaginary line at the foot of the x-height.

BASIC   An acronym formed from the words *B*eginner's *A*ll-purpose *S*ymbolic *I*nstruction *C*ode. A high-level programming language designed for use in a number of various forms for microcomputers. It is particularly suitable for entering and running programs on-line and is the most popular high-level language for microcomputers.

basis weight   (*US*) The weight of a ream (500 sheets) of paper cut to a given standard size, 25 x 38 inches for book papers.

bastard title   See **half-title.**

batter   A damaged or worn printing type or plate that therefore produces a defective impression.

battered   Used to describe a damaged or worn printing type or plate.

baud   Any of several units for measuring the rate at which data is transmitted, from one part of a computer system, e.g. a magnetic disk, to another part of the computer system, or between computers. Baud is used especially to refer to a measure of one unit of computer information (bit) per second.

BDG   Abbreviation of *binding*, response by a publisher to a bookseller to an order for a book that is not available. *BDG/9* (or *BDG/September*, *B/9*, or *B/September*) means Binding expected September; *BDG/ND* or *B/ND* means Binding, no date can be given.

bds   Abbreviation of *boards*, referring to a type of binding.

bear off   (*US*) To adjust the spacing in typeset text for justification.

bed   The flat surface of a letterpress printing press on which the type forme is placed in printing.

begin even   An instruction to a typesetter to set the text with lines starting at the margin, i.e. not indented.

bestseller   A book that has sold in great numbers, especially over a given, often short, period of time.

bf   Abbreviation of *bold face*; instruction to a typesetter to set the text in bold face.

bi-directional printing   The printing of lines both right to left and left to right, eliminating the need for a return to the beginning of the line. This speeds up the printing process.

Bible paper   A thin opaque paper that is used for books with many pages when lightness is required.

biblio   A page in the preliminary matter of a book, often the left-hand page after the title-page that gives information about the book's publisher, its publication date, the copyright notice, ISBN, name and address of printer, etc.

bibliography (1) A list of books on a particular subject for readers' further reference, usually part of the end matter of a book. (2) The study, description or knowledge of books, in regard to their outward form, authors, subjects, editions, and history.

binder's board (*US*) A fine-quality heavy cloth-covered board that is used to bind hardback books.

binder's brass A die made of brass or other metal that bears the design to be impressed into the cover of a book. US equivalent: *binder's die*.

binding The covering that fastens the pages of a book. There are a variety of binding methods, including **cased, perfect binding, saddle-stitch,** and **side-stitch.**

biography The description of a person's life written by another person.

bit An abbreviation from the words *bi*nary digi*t*. The smallest unit of information used in a computer, having one of two values, 1 or 0. The central processing unit of a computer is often described according to the number of bits that it can process or access at one time, e.g. 8 bit, 16 bit, or 32 bit CPUs. Computers usually store information as a series of bits.

bits per inch A measurement of the density of data on a storage medium. Also *bpi*.

bits per second The number of bits of information that can be passed through telecommunication equipment in one second. The higher the number, the more expensive the equipment and the faster the speed of transmission over long-distance connections. The lower the number, the cheaper the equipment, although charges for the telecommunication lines will rise because it will take more time to transmit or receive the same amount of information. Also *bps*.

black letter See **Gothic** (1).

black printer   (In colour reproduction) the black printing film and plate, used to increase the contrast of neutral tones and also to allow for foreign-language changes to the text.

blad   A sample booklet of part of a final book, used to promote the book at sales conferences, exhibitions, etc.

blanket   (In offset printing) a rubber or synthetic sheet wrapped round a cylinder (*the blanket cylinder*), to transfer the printing image from the plate to the paper.

blanket-to-blanket press   An offset printing press in which the two blanket cylinders act as impression cylinders to each other, the paper being printed on both sides at the same time.

bleed   (1) An illustration that extends beyond the trimmed size of a page in order to ensure that the print will run off the page after trimming.   (2) To bleed (or bleed off) is to extend an illustration beyond the trimmed size of a page.

blind blocking   The impressing of letters or a design on a book cover that produces a recessed surface which is not enhanced by the use of ink or metal foil.

blind P   The mark ¶ used to show a new paragraph.

blister pack   A display packet consisting of a transparent raised covering of clear plastic that is sealed to a backing board and encloses small retail items. Also known as **bubble pack.**

block   (In letterpress printing) a relief printing surface, from which an illustration or text is printed. In a line block, the design is represented by solid lines; in a half-tone block, the design is represented by a pattern of black dots of different sizes. US equivalent: *cut.*

block in   To sketch in the main outlines of a picture in preparing its design.

block letter   (1) A capital letter written in imitation of type. (2) A heavy-letter type, without serifs.

block out   To mask something, such as part of a negative, so that light does not pass through it.

blocking   (In bookbinding) the impressing of letters or a design on a book cover using ink or metal foil. US equivalent: *stamping*. See also **blind blocking.**

blow up   To make a photographic enlargement, the resulting photograph being called a blow-up.

blueprints; blues   See **Ozalid.**

blurb   A brief promotional description of a book, printed on the jacket or the back of the book.

board   A heavy paper or light card used for covers to catalogues and paperback books and also for cartons.

boards   Stiff material, as of pasteboard or pulp boards, used in bookbinding. In catalogues *boards* means that the book has a hardcover binding, with no jacket, but with the boards covered with an ornamental paper.

body   (1) The rectangular piece of metal that carries a character from which an inked print can be made. See also **body size.**   (2) The main part of a book, excluding the preliminary pages, footnotes, endmatter, etc.

body copy; body matter   The main text of a work, excluding the headings.

body size   The measurement of the type body from back to front, i.e. from top to bottom when looking at the printing surface. The body size remains the same throughout a particular fount and is measured in points. Type can also be cast on a larger body, e.g. 10pt on 11pt, to produce the same space between lines as a separate 1pt lead.

body type   (*US*) The type used for setting the main part of the text of a work, in contrast to the type for headings.

BOGOFF   Abbreviation of *buy one get one for free*, a selling strategy in which on the purchase of one item, the customer receives another free of charge.

bold face A typeface which appears with blacker, heavier strokes than normal and is used for emphasis, e.g. in headings. Bold face is shown on a manuscript by a wavy underlining.

bolts The outer edges of a folded sheet or section before the book is trimmed.

bond A quality of evenly finished paper generally used for letterheads in a range of weights from $63\,gm^2$ to $120\,gm^2$, but usually $80\,gm^2$.

book A work consisting of a number of pages bound together.

book block (In perfect binding and in cased binding) the trimmed and glued or sewn sections of a book, before the cover is fitted in place.

book club An organisation that sells normally specially produced low-priced editions of books to its members by mail order. Members of a book club are usually committed to buying a minimum number of books.

book paper A general classification for coated and uncoated papers suitable for book printing.

book proof A proof showing the pages in correct order, often without the illustrations.

book review A critical examination of a book, printed in a newspaper, magazine, etc.

book sizes The following list gives the trimmed page size in millimetres, according to the metric system, as used in Britain. Measurements are height × width:

Metric crown 8vo	186×123
Metric crown 4to	246×189
Metric large crown 8vo	198×129
Metric large crown 4to	258×201
Metric demy 8vo	216×138
Metric demy 4to	276×219
Metric royal 8vo	234×156
Metric royal 4to	312×237

US book sizes, in inches, measurements being width × height:

5½ × 8½	6⅛ × 9¼
5 × 7⅜	5⅜ × 8
5½ × 8¼	5⅝ × 8⅜

book token A card bearing a special voucher that can be used in payment or exchange for a book to the stated value.

bookbinding See **binding.**

booklet A short publication that is saddle-stitched and has a limp cover.

bookplate A label that is pasted inside the cover of a book, usually bearing the owner's name, crest, coat-of-arms, etc.

bookseller A person who retails books to the public and public institutions; the owner or manager of a bookshop.

bootstrap A method of inputting data prior to the loading of a computer program in order that the program can be loaded.

border A continuous ornamental design or line that is arranged around the text on a page.

bottom out (*US*) To arrange the text on a page so that there are no unsightly divisions at the bottom of a page or widows.

box A section of printed matter, especially a special feature, that is separated from the main text and illustrations on all four sides by a line.

box head The heading of a particular column of information that is arranged in a table.

bpi Abbreviation of *bits per inch*, a measurement for the density of data on a storage medium.

bps Abbreviation of *bits per second*, the number of bits of information that can be passed through telecommunication equipment in one second.

brace   The sign } used to connect words, lines, figures, staves of music, etc., indicating that they are to be taken together.

brackets   The general name for the marks used to enclose words or mathematical symbols. Printers and typesetters consider brackets to be *square brackets*. See also **angle brackets; brace; parentheses; square brackets.**

brass   See **binder's brass.**

break-even point   The point at which the publisher's receipts from the sale of a particular number of copies of a book cover the investment costs on that book.

break off   An instruction to a typesetter or printer to begin the text on the next line rather than run it on to the present line.

breve   The curved mark ˘ used to indicate a short vowel or syllable.

Bristol board   A smooth fine-quality cardboard made in various thicknesses, used for printing and drawing.

broad fold   The folding of paper in which the pattern of fibres in the paper runs along the shorter length after folding.

broadsheet   Also known as **broadside** (1) A large sheet of paper that is not folded or cut. The term is commonly used to refer to a newspaper with a large format, approximately 15in × 24in (380 × 610 mm).   (2) A large single sheet of advertising, printed on one side only.

brochure   A short work, especially one that contains advertising or information. Brochures are unbound and saddle-stitched.

bromide   A photograph of printed matter, printed on a special photographic paper that is coated with silver bromide emulsion. Bromides are used in phototypesetting, reproduction, and photography.

bronzing   A method of obtaining a metallic lustre. The printed matter is first printed with an adhesive ink and then bronze powder is dusted on.

bubble   An approximately circular enclosure of the words or thoughts of a character in a cartoon.

bubble pack   See **blister pack.**

buckram   A coarse cotton or linen fabric that is stiffened and used in library bindings or binding large heavy books.

bug   An error or defect in a computer system or computer program.

bulk   (1) The estimated thickness of a book, excluding the cover, enabling the jacket to be designed with the correct width of spine.   (2) The measured thickness of paper relative to its weight. In the USA bulk is expressed as a *bulk factor*, the number of pages that make a thickness of one inch.   (3) The main part of the delivery of finished copies of a book by a printer.

bullet   A solid round dot ● used to precede items in a list or to highlight particular points in a text. The bullet is used especially in advertisements and promotions.

by-line   A line printed with a newspaper or magazine article or photograph that gives the author's or photographer's name.

Cc

©   Symbol for **copyright.**

c and lc   Abbreviation of *capital(s) and lower case*, instruction to a typesetter to set in large and small letters.

C series; C sizes   A series of metric paper sizes, used for envelopes or folders suitable for stationery and papers in the A sizes. The sizes are:

C0	917 mm × 1297 mm
C1	648 mm × 917 mm
C2	458 mm × 648 mm
C3	324 mm × 458 mm
C4	229 mm × 324 mm
C5	162 mm × 229 mm
C6	114 mm × 162 mm
C7	81 mm × 114 mm
C7/6	81 mm × 162 mm
DL	110 mm × 220 mm

CAD   Abbreviation of *computer aided design.* The use of computers to aid design involving computer graphics, modelling, simulation, and analysis of designs for production.

CAD/CAM   Abbreviation of *computer aided design and manufacture.* The use of computers to aid design and manufacturing processes. It can also include robotics and automated testing procedures.

calender   To press paper through a stack of rollers (a calender stack) that polish the paper and give it a smooth finish.

calligraphy   The art of producing fine handwriting.

18

camera-ready copy   Positive matter that is ready to be photographed for platemaking. Also *CRC*. Also known as **camera ready.**

cancel   A new reprinted leaf to be substituted for a suppressed leaf (containing a major error) after the book is printed.

cap height   The vertical distance of a capital letter from top to bottom. The highest point may be below the top of an ascender; the lowest point will be on the base line.

cap line   The imaginary horizontal line that runs across the highest point of capital letters.

capital   A large letter: A, in contrast to a, and small capitals: A. Capitals are shown on a manuscript, galley proof, etc., by three lines under the relevant characters. Also known as **upper case.**

caps   Abbreviation of *capitals* (upper-case letters).

caps and s.c.   Abbreviation of *capitals and small capitals*, instruction to a typesetter, to set the (lower-case) text in small capitals and the initial letters in capitals. Also known as **caps and smalls.**

caption   (1) The descriptive heading or accompanying wording of an illustration. (2) The heading of an article, chapter, or section.

carbon paper   A thin sheet of paper that is coated on one side with a waxy pigment. When a sheet of carbon paper is placed between two sheets of paper, the pressure of writing or typing on the top sheet transfers an exact copy to the bottom sheet.

carbonless paper   Paper which has been chemically impregnated so that when the top sheet is struck an image is produced on second and subsequent sheets without the use of interleaved carbon paper. See also **NCR.**

cardboard   A stiff board made from paper pulp, used for making boxes and packaging materials.

caret　The symbol ⟨ used to show the insertion of something omitted.

carriage return　A key on an electronic typewriter or computer keyboard which when depressed ends a line of type and returns the cursor or the printing point to the start of the next line.

cartridge paper　A firm strong paper with a rough surface, used for drawing and printing.

case　(1) The hard covers of a book, i.e. the front, back, and spine.　(2) The sectioned tray in which type is contained for hand composition. This is the origin of the terms *upper case* and *lower case*.

cased; casebound　Bound in hard, especially cloth-covered boards.

casing in　The applying of a case (a hardback binding) to a book.

cast　To mould or shape an individual character. In hot-metal composition, molten metal is forced into a matrix to make the character.

cast-coated paper　A type of coated paper, made by drying under pressure against a polished drum, to give a very glossy enamel finish.

cast-off　An estimate of the length of copy, including number of words, illustrations, etc., expressed in the number of pages the copy will fill when printed.

cataloguing in publication　See **CIP data**.

catchword; catchphrase　(1) A word or phrase in the text, e.g. an entry in a dictionary, which is repeated at the top of the column containing the entry.　(2) A word or phrase repeated at the beginning of a textual note at the bottom of the page.

CD-ROM　Abbreviation of *Compact Disc–Read Only Memory*, a method of storing a large amount of information on compact disc. By means of a CD-ROM drive (or player), a computer, monitor, and printer, users can interact with the data on the compact disc, drive the system, and find and work interactively with the required information quickly.

cedilla A mark placed under the letter 'c' to indicate an s-sound (in French and Portuguese), and in other languages, e.g. Turkish, to denote other sounds.

cellulose acetate A sheet of synthetic material, usually transparent or translucent, that is used for overlays to artwork; it is also used in photographic films.

centre To align a line of type so that the middle of the line is at the centre of the specified width.

centre spread The centre facing two pages of a section.

centred point A raised dot, centred on the x-height, used as a decimal point in numbers. US equivalent: *centered dot*.

chain lines The lines running across laid paper, impressed by a dandy roll in a papermaking machine.

chapter drop The level at which the main text starts at the beginning of a chapter, section, etc.

character Any letter of the alphabet, number, symbol, or punctuation mark in typesetting.

character count The total number of characters in a particular text.

character reader A device that automatically inputs printed characters into a computer. Also known as **optical character reader.**

character recognition The use of recognition techniques so that a character reader can identify characters, usually alphanumeric. There are several types of technique, e.g. **magnetic-ink character recognition; optical character recognition.**

character set The collection of numbers, letters, and symbols in a particular fount.

chart Information arranged in the form of a table, diagram or graph.

chase (In letterpress printing) the rectangular metal frame into which type and blocks are fitted and secured for printing.

cheap edition The re-issue of an already published book in a different form, for example on cheaper paper and with a cheaper binding.

chemical pulping (In papermaking) the treatment of chipped wood with chemicals to remove lignin, resins, etc.

chipboard A board made by consolidating wood pulp, waste materials, etc., with a synthetic resin.

chromo A type of smooth paper, coated on one side, and used for posters, proofs, and the printing of labels.

cicero A European measure of the type, one cicero being equal to 4.511 mm (0.1776 in) or 12 Didot points.

CIF; c i f Abbreviation of *cost, insurance, and freight*. A term used in the preparation of export documents which indicates that the purchaser is responsible for paying the cost of the goods, insurance against risk and freight charges, whether the goods are sent by sea or air.

CIP data Abbreviation of *Cataloguing in Publication data*, information in a scheme operated by the British Library and the Library of Congress. These institutions prepare classified entries for a particular book, showing its title, author, library cataloguing classifications, ISBN, etc. The information is printed on the biblio page of a book.

circumflex The accent ˆ.

clean (Of proofs) having few errors.

close up An instruction to delete a space between characters or lines.

cloth The material used to cover the boards of a case in binding a book.

cloth-lined board   The cover of a book, in which one side has been lined with cloth or linen to give greater strength.

club line   The unsightly first line of a paragraph that appears at the foot of a page.

co-edition   An edition of a book that is published simultaneously by two or more publishers in different languages or in different markets. Production costs are therefore shared.

co-publishing   The arrangement to publish a co-edition of a book. See **co-edition.**

coated paper   Paper that has a coating of a mineral which gives a smooth finish. Quality half-tone illustrations, for example, should be printed on coated art paper. US equivalent: *enamel paper.*

cold composition; cold type   Typesetting by photographic methods, i.e. filmsetting or photocomposition or by typewriter, in contrast with *hot-metal typesetting.*

collate   (1) To place in order, as sheets of a book (or gathered sections) for binding, and to examine with respect to completeness and sequence of sheets. US equivalent: *conflate.*   (2) To examine and compare books, and especially old manuscripts, in order to ascertain information about the history of composition and publication.

collating machine   A device used in the production of multiple copies of documents. As documents are copied, a collating machine bundles each document set together in chronological order of copying. In more expensive machines, an attachment for stapling, binding, etc., completed sets is incorporated into the collator.

collation marks   Marks printed where the final fold of a section of a book comes. The marks usually appear in a staggered sequence so that it can be readily seen if any are missing or out of order.

collotype A planographic printing process using a flat surface of gelatine, used particularly in fine-art reproductions of short runs.

colophon An inscription at the end of a book or literary composition, often naming the author and scribe or printer, with place and date of execution, etc., as on a modern title-page.

colour bar (In four-colour processing) a set of bars on proofs, used to check the quality and strength of colours on the proof.

colour chart A chart showing combinations of the three process colours, yellow, magenta, and cyan, enabling the choice of coloured inks or tints.

colour control bar A coloured strip with different densities beyond the printed area of a photograph, used to show the printer the nature of each colour film.

colour correction The adjustment of colour values to improve the reproduction of an image, by, for example, adjusting colour filters or the colour scanner.

colour filter A thin layer of coloured glass, plastic, or gelatine, placed over a camera lens to allow the transmission of certain colours or wavelengths; used in correcting and separating colours.

colour separation The breaking-up of original colours of an image into four component colours, magenta, cyan, yellow, and black, by using colour filters in a camera or an electronic scanner. The colour-separation process results in four pieces of film, one for each colour.

column A vertical section of a page containing text or a table of figures or other information.

column inch/centimetre A unit of measure of printed text, especially advertising in a newspaper or magazine, one column in width by one inch/centimetre in depth.

column rule The light vertical line that is used to separate columns in a newspaper or magazine.

comb binding See **mechanical binding.**

combination line and half-tone A combination of line artwork (text that is black on white, with no intermediate tones) and half-tones (photographs represented by a pattern of black dots), used for example where text is to be superimposed on photographs.

commercial a The sign @ used in calculating prices, to mean 'at'.

commission (1) Money paid to a salesman or agent who brings about a sale, usually expressed as a percentage of the price paid. (2) To assign a particular task to an author, editor, artist, etc.

comp (1) Abbreviation of **compositor.** (2) Abbreviation of **comprehensive.**

compatibility The ability of two devices whether hardware or software to work in conjuction, e.g. if a magnetic disk used on one computer can be read by another computer, the two computers are said to be compatible. Computer compatibility usually means software compatibility. If a program can be run on two computers without alteration to the program, the computers are said to be compatible.

compiler The person who selects or collects material for an anthology, book of quotations, etc.

complimentary copy A copy of a book sent free, traditionally as one of six to the author, or to a lecturer, teacher, etc., for his or her recommendation to students.

compose To set type by machine or by hand.

composing room The part of a printer's establishment where text is typeset and arranged.

composition The type has been set in a form that is ready to be reproduced.

composition size A size of type up to 14 points, used for setting text in a book. The term derives from the tradition in hot-metal typesetting of setting sizes up to 14 points on a composing machine.

compositor   A person who sets type. US equivalent: *typographer*.

comprehensive   (*US*) See **visual.**

computer graphics   The production of drawings, photographs, text, etc., of a book by using computers, e.g. to overlap pictures, produce montages, and increase the height of images.

computerised composition; computerised typesetting   The use of computers to perform various aspects of the composition and typesetting processes. A text may be keyboarded, with codes, as continuous copy. The computer, programmed with the necessary specifications to carry out the tasks, will produce hyphenated justified text according to a particular page format, for output on a disk or tape or for direct input to the phototypesetter.

concertina fold   A special fold used for pamphlets in which each fold goes in the opposite direction to the previous one. US equivalent: *accordion fold.*

condensed   A narrow typeface.

conflate   (*US*) See **collate** (1).

contact print   A photographic print made with the negative in direct contact with the sensitised paper, film, or plate.

contents   The page at the beginning of a book listing the book's chapters, sections, articles, etc.

continuous tone   A photograph or illustration that contains continuous shades of light and dark tone values that are not broken up into dots.

contract   An agreement between two parties such as a publisher and author or a publisher and another publisher. In the contract, the obligations of both parties are set out, e.g. the tasks to be done, the schedule for delivery of the work, the payments to be made, the ownership of copyright, and the apportionment of earnings from the sale of rights.

contrast   The degree of variation of tone or density between the lightest and darkest parts of a picture, especially a photograph.

copperplate printing   An intaglio printing process in which a polished copper plate is engraved or etched with a design.

copy   Material to be printed, e.g. typescripts, photographs, and line drawings.

copy-editing   The preparation of a manuscript for typesetting, including correcting linguistic usage, spelling, and styling according to the publisher's guidelines.

copy fitting   The estimation of the size of type and width of a line necessary to fit a text into a particular extent.

copy holder   (1) A piece of equipment which is used to hold text upright for ease in keying into a computer in a position near to the screen and keyboard and adjustable for the comfort of the operator.   (2) (In former use) an assistant who reads material aloud that is being checked by a proofreader.

copy preparation   The marking-up of a manuscript with the typographical specifications chosen by the designer.

copying machine   A machine that will reproduce an exact copy of an original document through the action of heat, electrostatic charge, or light. See also **photocopier.**

copyright   The legal and exclusive right of an originator of a work, photograph, illustration, etc., to reproduce that work unless he or she gives permission to another. Copyright is regulated by national laws and international conventions.

copyright deposit The supply, obligatory in some countries, of a copy or copies of every published item to a central office.

corner marks The marks on a piece of paper indicating where the paper is to be trimmed or cut or used on overlays, artwork, film, etc., to position the work correctly.

corrigenda A list of corrections printed in a book, especially in contrast to an errata slip that is pasted or placed into a book.

costing The estimate of the cost of a particular product or process. For example, a publisher will take into account the cost of services, materials, etc., that can be directly attributed to each title and also the general expenditure that cannot be directly attributed to a book (overheads).

counterpack A table-top display box holding small quantities of goods.

cover The paper, board, cloth, etc., to which the main part of a book is attached.

cover paper A strong thick paper, usually coloured, used especially for the covers of pamphlets and brochures.

cpi Abbreviation of *characters per inch*, in a designer's specification, estimates of the length of a manuscript, and also in specifying the number of characters to every (horizontal) inch of typing.

cpl Abbreviation of *characters per line*, in a designer's specification, estimates of the length of a manuscript, and in specifying the number of characters per line of typing.

cps Abbreviation of *characters per second,* the speed of a printer being measured by how many characters (letters, numbers, or symbols) the printer can transfer to paper every second.

CRC Abbreviation of *camera-ready copy*, positive matter that is ready to be photographed for platemaking.

crease To impress a mark on board or thicker paper to make the folding easier.

credit An acknowledgment of the organisation or person that has provided an illustration, photograph, etc. Also known as **credit line.**

Cromalin A form of **dry proofing** system.

crop marks Guidelines showing which parts of an illustration are not to be reproduced, placed outside the area that is to be reproduced.

cropping Cutting off or masking the areas of an illustration which are not to be reproduced.

cross-reference An instruction at one place in a book to direct a reader to another part of the book for further relevant information.

crosshead A centred heading for a subsection or paragraph.

crown See **book sizes; paper sizes.**

Crown copyright The legal and exclusive right to material published by government departments. It is illegal to reproduce it without prior permission.

CTN Abbreviation of *confectioners, tobacconists, and newsagents*, a group of retail shops.

cursive A typeface that imitates handwriting in which the characters are joined in each word.

cursor A marker on a VDU indicating the point at which text should be entered. Some cursors are boxes, triangles, or underlines, and some flash on and off.

cut (*US*) See **block.**

cut and paste A word processing term. Often an operator will find that the layout of text in a document needs to be changed. Instead of deleting and re-entering the text, the operator can mark the text to be repositioned (cut) and move it to a new location (paste). A labour-saving feature when large blocks of text have to be moved. The term derives from the actual cutting and pasting of text.

cut edges The three edges of a book that are trimmed with a guillotine.

cut marks (*US*) The marks on a printed sheet to show where the paper is to be trimmed.

cylinder press (In letterpress printing) a printing machine in which the forme (the frame containing the metal type) is carried on a flat bed under a revolving cylinder. The paper to be printed is carried on the cylinder which presses it on to the inked forme to make an impression.

Cyrillic Of the alphabet used for writing languages such as Russian and Bulgarian.

Dd

dagger   The character † used as a (second-level) reference mark, especially to a footnote.

daisy wheel   A type of flat circular printing head on a word processor, etc., with the characters attached round it on the ends of the 'stalks'.

daisy wheel printer   A printer which makes use of a daisy wheel. The wheel rotates at speed until the required character is brought before a hammer. The character is then struck by the hammer against the ribbon. Daisy wheels are interchangeable to facilitate different typefaces and produce letter-quality print-out.

dandy roll   (In papermaking) a wire-covered roller that comes into contact with the wet paper, compresses the pulp, squeezes out water, and impresses watermarks and laid lines into the texture.

dash   A punctuation mark—commonly known as an **em rule.**

data   Characters or numbers that provide the building blocks for information. Data is normally deemed to be input into a computer in order that information can be output.

data processing   Clerical, arithmetical, and logical operations on data. In the context of information technology, data processing implies the use of a computer in its operations. Also known as **DP.**

databank   A large collection of information stored in a computer, which can process it and from which particular items of information can be retrieved when required.

database   An organised collection of files of information that has been systematically recorded. The files can be interconnected and form the base of an organisation's data processing system, with specific reference to information retrieval.

de-luxe edition   A more luxurious edition of a book than the standard edition, printed on higher-quality paper and given a lavish elegant binding.

deadline   The date before which a particular task must be completed, for example the time after which material for an issue of a newspaper or magazine will not be accepted.

debug   To test a computer program or routine and to isolate and correct errors to remove bugs or faults.

decimal point   The full stop or raised full stop that separates the unit and the decimal fraction.

deckle   (1) The width of a papermaking machine. (2) Either of the straps along the edges of the wire of a paper machine, so fixing the width of the *web* (paper). Also known as **deckle strap.**

deckle edge   The rough untrimmed edge, especially on hand-made paper, caused by the deckle or produced artificially.

dedicated   (Of a program procedure, machine, network channel or system) set apart for a special use. Often the term is used to refer to word processors which will only do word processing, i.e. they are dedicated to word processing.

dedication   The author's inscription of the book to another person, part of the preliminary pages to a book, especially the recto page immediately following the title-page.

deep-etch   To remove the unwanted parts from a half-tone plate by etching, to leave a white background.

delete   To remove.

delivery   The passing of a manuscript by an author to a publisher, of copies of books by a printer to a publisher, etc.

delivery note   A list of goods delivered, given to the customer with the goods, also the document that is signed by the person receiving the goods, confirming their safe delivery.

demy   See **book sizes; paper sizes.**

density   (1) The degree of tone or colour, especially darkness, of an image.   (2) (Of type) the degree of compactness within a particular area of text.

descender   The part of a lower-case letter that extends below the bottom of the letter *x*, for example *p, q*. Contrast with *ascender*.

design   The planning and arrangement of the form of publications, including format, typography, photography, and illustrations.

desktop publishing   An office system made up of a personal computer, the necessary software, and a laser printer, used to produce printed material, including text and graphics.

device   An ornamental design or emblem, of for example a publisher, that may be part of the **colophon.**

Dewey decimal classification   A decimal system of classifying library books based on ten main subject areas that are divided up, with further subdivisions as necessary.

diacritical marks   Accents, cedillas, and other marks attached to letters to indicate modified sound, value, etc.

diaeresis   Two dots placed over the second of two adjacent vowels to show that each is to be pronounced separately, e.g. in *naïve*.

diazo paper   See **dyeline process.**

dictionary   A small additional program available on some word processing packages which will check edited text for spelling errors against an inbuilt dictionary in the program. Ready-made dictionaries can be purchased, many of which can be added to if the user requires the addition of specialised words.

Didot   A European system of measuring type, measuring 0.0148 in (0.376 mm). 12 Didot points = 4.511 mm. See also **cicero; point.**

die cutting   The use of a cutting and creasing device to cut paper, card, etc., into special shapes, used mainly for cartons.

die stamping   An intaglio printing process in which all the printed characters of the impression are in relief, used for letterheads, cards, etc.

digitise   To put data into a digital form (numerically, as separate pulses) that can be processed electronically.

diphthong   The representation of two vowel-sounds pronounced as one syllable, also often applied to two letters joined together and printed as one character, e.g. *æ*. See also **ligature.**

direct costs   Costs that are directly related to a particular task, e.g. work on a particular title, in contrast to general overhead business costs (*indirect costs*).

direct input   A keyboarding device that inserts text directly into a computerised typesetting system and output device.

direct process   A method of photocopying that uses paper which has been specially treated with a photoconductive coating. In the photocopier, the paper is given an electrostatic charge and then exposed to a light source, enabling an invisible charged image of the original to be retained on the paper. This image attracts fine particles of developer (either liquid or powder) and the image of the original appears on the paper. Compare with *indirect process*.

dirty   (Of proofs) having many corrections.

discount   The reduction of a full price to a buyer by a seller, as the difference, usually expressed as a percentage, between the price at which a bookseller sells a book and the price at which the bookseller has to buy the book from the publisher. The discount can vary with the type of book, quantity ordered, etc.

discretionary hyphen   In keyboarding, a hyphen inserted into a word by the keyboard operator when it is foreseen that the hyphenation logic of the machine will result in unsatisfactory hyphenation. A discretionary hyphen remains suppressed unless it is required.

disk   A flat circular medium used for magnetic backing storage of information and programs. A disk is divided into recording tracks and subdivided into sectors. Each track and sector is addressable, which gives disk storage its random access capability, enabling programs and data to be accessed or retrieved quickly.

disk drive   An electro-mechanical device, attached to a computer, phototypesetter, etc., that houses a magnetic disk effecting necessary movement and writing to or reading from the disk.

disk operating system   Software that manages the storage and retrieval of information on disk and controls the operation of all activities relating to the use of magnetic disks in a computer system. Also known as **DOS.**

display   (1) The production of a visual record on a television (or similar) screen, the term being sometimes used to apply to the screen itself.   (2) The layout of a document (letter, memorandum, etc.) with regard to indentations.

display matter   Large typefaces, especially larger than 14 points, used for title pages, headings. Also known as **display size; display type.**

displayed   (Of text, such as long quotations) set on separate lines, indented and preceded and followed by extra space to distinguish it from the rest of the text.

diss   Abbreviation of **distribute.**

distribute   To put (hand-set) type back into its correct position in its case, or to melt down machine-set type.

distribution   The sending of goods from manufacturers to consumers; in publishing, from publishers, sometimes via wholesalers, to bookshops and from there to the general public.

ditto marks   The marks „ used to show repetition of a word, number, etc., directly above in the previous line.

doctor blade   (In gravure printing) a thin flexible steel blade that is drawn across the surface of the plate or cylinder to remove surplus ink from the non-printing areas.

DOS   Abbreviation of *disk operating system*, software that manages the storage and retrieval of information on disk.

dot   The basic individual element in a half-tone.

dot etching   A method of adjusting the size of dots on half-tones. To increase a colour, the dot size is etched (reduced) on a negative; to decrease a colour, the dot size is etched on a positive.

dot-for-dot   Of the further reproduction of half-tone prints that have already been screened.

dot gain   A printing defect in which the size of half-tones increases slightly.

dot-matrix printer   A printer in which each character is made up of a series of dots produced by a print head pushing a pattern of wires against a ribbon and on to the paper; the head also moves across the paper.

double   (1) A word, section, etc., that is wrongly repeated.   (2) A size of paper twice the normal size. The size is taken by doubling the shorter side of the standard sheet, e.g. demy 17½in × 22½in, double demy 22½in × 35in.

double dagger   The character ‡ used as a (third-level) reference mark, especially to a footnote.

double-page spread   The two facing pages of a publication, as used for an illustration across the two pages.

draft   To prepare a basic outline, a plan, or a rough version of text, an illustration, etc.

drawn-on   (Of a book cover) attached to the sewn or perfect-bound book by gluing the spine.

drive out   To arrange the text with a wide word spacing to increase the number of lines the text occupies.

drop cap   A large initial capital letter at the beginning of text, especially a chapter, that extends over two or three lines of the text below. Also known as **drop initial.**

drop folio   A page number printed at the foot of the page.

drop-out blue   A light blue marker that does not reproduce, used to write directions on artwork.

dropped head   The beginning of a text, especially a chapter, that is set lower than the first line of the text on other pages.

drum printer   A type of line printer which prints from a drum engraved with identical characters in each print position across the drum, with a full set of characters engraved in each print position around the drum.

dry ink   (In some photocopiers) the powder that is used to produce the image; toner.

dry mounting   The use of heat-sensitive adhesives in mounting items to be photographed.

dry offset   See **letterset.**

dry proofing   The process of providing a colour proof that uses a toner powder or coloured film rather than ink.

dry-transfer lettering   Lettering on the back of a plastic sheet that can be rubbed down onto paper, etc., when preparing artwork.

DTP   Abbreviation of **desktop publishing.**

dual spectrum   A method of photocopying which produces a negative first by exposing the original document and the sensitised side of special paper to a light source. The negative is then used by the machine to produce the finished copy similar to a photograph. This process allows for colour copying.

dues   Books that have been ordered but which are not available immediately from the publisher. The publisher records the orders and processes them once the books become available.

dummy   A sample of a proposed job made up with the actual material and cut to the correct size to show bulk, style of binding, etc.

dumpbin   A low open container in which packets of goods are heaped in a shop, in order to draw attention to a special offer or to gain impulse buys.

duodecimo   (1) Having 12 leaves to the sheet, usually written 12mo.   (2) A book, or the size of a book, made up of such sheets.

duotone   A two-colour half-tone printed from two negatives.

duplex board/paper   Board/paper of two qualities or colours pasted together, usually by lamination, the result having a different colour or finish on each side.

duplicate   (1) To make one or more copies of an original document, using spirit, stencil (or ink), or offset litho duplicators.   (2) An exact copy of an original.

duplicator   A generic term which identifies one of the following: spirit duplicator, ink (or stencil) duplicator, or offset litho duplicator, all of which are used in the reproduction of multiple-copy documents.

dust cover; dust jacket   The removable paper cover of a book.

dyeline process   A copying process in which the copying paper (diazo paper) is coated with a compound that contains a light-sensitive dye. As light passes through the original to the diazo sheet, the compound is decomposed, leaving a positive original. The copy is developed in an ammonia vapour or other chemical.

Ee

E & OE   Abbreviation of *errors and omissions excepted*, a term included on invoices to mean that if the supplier has made any errors on the invoice, the details may be altered to the correct ones.

EAN   Abbreviation of *European Article Number*; see **bar code.**

editing   The preparation of a manuscript for publication. See also **copy-editing.**

edition   The number of copies of a book printed at a time, or at different times without significant alteration.

editorial work   The activities of a publisher concerned with the preparation of a text for publication, including the commissioning or choosing of manuscripts, working with authors, gaining permission to use copyright material, checking that publication of the material would not result in libel, breach of copyright, etc., and the preparation of manuscripts for typesetting.

educational contractor   A supplier who provides an educational institution, especially a school, with textbooks and other educational materials.

electro   (In letterpress printing) a printing plate made by electrolytically coating a mould with copper. Also known as **electrotype.**

electrostatic   Of a printing or copying process that uses stationary electric charges to attract ink (toner) to an image on a printing surface. See also **xerographic copier.**

elision   The omission of something considered inessential, especially in numbers, for example 67–69 becoming 67–9 and 424–427 becoming 424–27.

elite   A measurement of typewriter typesize, twelve characters to the horizontal inch.

ellipsis   Three dots indicating the omission of a word or words.

em   (1) The square of the body of any size of type, used as a measurement. The name em comes from the area of metal body of the letter *M*. Also known as **mutton.**   (2) The standard unit of measurement of typeset material, 4.23 mm (about one-sixth of an inch) or 12 points. Also known as **pica em; pica.**

em rule   A rule which occupies the width of an em or the square of any size of type; dash.

embossing   The raising of lettering above the surface of paper, cloth, etc., in relief printing.

emulsion   A light-sensitive coating on a photographic material.

en   Half of an em, regarded as the average width of characters and used in typesetters' calculations of the extent of a text. Also known as **nut.**

en point   A point which is placed in the middle of a piece of type as wide as an en so that it is printed with space on either side.

en rule   A rule which is half the width of an em rule, used for example as the short dash in: 1939–45. Also known as **en dash.**

enamel paper   (*US*) See **coated paper.**

end even   An instruction to a typesetter that the final part of the text to be set should be a complete line.

end-of-line decisions   The decisions on where to hyphenate words and how the text should be justified. See **hyphenation and justification.**

endmatter   The parts of a book which follow the text (e.g. appendices, bibliography, index). US equivalent: *back matter.*

endnotes Notes which come at the end of the relevant chapter or at the end of the book instead of being printed at the foot of the relevant page.

endpaper A folded sheet at the beginning or end of a book, one leaf of which is pasted to the binding, leaving the other as a flyleaf.

engraving (1) The etching of a design onto a steel or copper plate to create a recessed image. (2) A print made from an engraved plate.

enlargement The process of making a photograph, illustration, etc., larger in reproduction; the amount by which the photograph, etc., is made larger.

ennage The total number of ens in a text to be set.

epigraph A quotation or motto at the beginning of a book or a chapter.

EPROM Abbreviation of *erasable programmable read only memory*. A chip containing a program which it will hold until it is erased by exposing the surface of the chip to ultra-violet light. The chip has the facility to be reprogrammed.

EROM Abbreviation of *erasable read only memory*. A chip containing a computer program which will hold it until it is erased by exposing the surface of the chip to ultra-violet light.

errata slip A list of corrections or errors in writing or printing, pasted or placed into a book.

escalator clause A section of a contract that grants a higher rate of payment for sales beyond a stated figure, usually except on small reprints.

esparto A strong grass used to make a high-quality smooth opaque bulky paper.

estimate An estimate of the cost of producing a book, especially the price quoted by a printer for a particular job.

etching   (1) The production of a design on metal, glass, etc., by the action of a corrosive chemical, especially an acid.   (2) A print taken from an etched plate.

even pages   The left-hand (verso) pages, i.e. those with even numbers.

even small caps   Small capital letters for all the letters of a word, without using a full capital for the beginning of a word.

even working   The production of a book in which the book can be completed using full sheets of paper, especially in sections of 32 pages.

exception dictionary   (In computerised typesetting) a program that lists words that do not conform to the standard word-break rules.

expanded type   A typeface which is wider than usual to give an oblong, flattened form.

exposure   The subjection of a sensitive photographic film, plate, etc., to light, equalling the intensity of light multiplied by the duration of the exposure.

extent   The length of a book measured in number of pages.

extract   Material that is quoted from another book, magazine, etc., especially when the quotation is indented from the main text or set in a smaller typeface than the rest of the text.

Ff

f and c/f and g   Abbreviation of **folded and collated/ gathered.**

face   (1) The printing surface of a piece of type.   (2) See **typeface.**

face out   (Of books) displayed on a shelf with the front cover facing outwards.

facsimile transmission   A means of transmitting a *facsimile* (exact copy) of a document to a distant point over telephone lines. The equipment at the sending and receiving points must be compatible. The document is scanned by a device (like a copier) and the image is converted, via a modem into electronic digital form and is then reconverted at the distant point to recreate the image on paper as hard copy. Also known as **fax.**

fade-out half-tone   (*US*) See **vignette** (2).

family   A group of related characters of the same design but with italic, bold, condensed, etc., founts, and in different sizes.

fascicle   One part of a book issued in parts. Also known as **fascicule.**

fax   Abbreviation for **facsimile transmission** or facsimile communication.

featherweight paper   A light but bulky paper, used to make a large book with few pages, e.g. in children's picture books.

fee   The single payment made for a particular service, especially to an illustrator, writer of a foreword, etc., but also sometimes to an author, instead of a royalty.

feint   Used to describe the thin horizontal pale blue lines on paper in exercise books, account books, etc., used as a guide to writing.

felt side   The top smoother side of paper that is uppermost in the manufacture of paper.

fiction   The class of literature consisting of books, especially novels, containing imaginary invented stories.

figure   (1) An illustration in the text.   (2) A number; used by some printers to refer specifically to Arabic numerals.

figure number   The reference number of a particular illustration.

file   To submit copy to a newspaper.

filler   Material such as an article or illustration used to fill space in a column or page in a newspaper, magazine, etc.

film   Positive or negative photographic film, from which plates are made.

film assembly   The collection and correct positioning of all the type, illustrations, etc., on a page for photographing the camera-ready copy and platemaking.

film speeds   A numerical expression of the sensitivity of a particular film to light, given as an ASA (American Standards Association) or DIN (Deutsche Industrie Norm) number.

filmsetting   See **phototypesetting.**

filter   A thin layer of glass, plastic, or gelatine, placed over a camera lens to allow the transmission of certain colours or wavelengths.

fine rule   A very thin line.

finish   The surface of paper, especially regarding its texture or appearance.

finishing The set of processes in book production after the pages of a book have been printed. Finishing includes cutting, scoring, and folding the pages and binding, and sometimes also addressing and mailing.

firm On terms that cannot be changed. Used with reference to the supply of books to a bookseller to mean that books will be paid for at the agreed price within a given time and that they cannot be returned without first obtaining the publisher's permission.

fist The mark ☞ used to direct the reader to a reference note, different section, etc. Also known as **index.**

fixative A clear varnish that is sprayed over drawings or artwork to give a protective coating.

fixed space A standard unvariable space between words or characters, used especially in unjustified text.

flag (1) Information that can be added to computer data in order to characterise the data or to provide information about it. (2) A marker attached to a sheet of paper. (3) See **masthead.**

flap The inside fold of a book jacket. Information printed on the flap includes a description of the book, its author, and the book's price.

flash An additional exposure in half-tone photography to strengthen the density of dots in the dark areas.

flat (1) (Of a photograph or half-tone) lacking in contrast. (2) A composite assembly of negatives in position, with cut-out windows that allow light to pass through the image areas during exposure.

flat-bed press A printing machine in which the forme is carried on a horizontal bed under a revolving cylinder. See **cylinder press.**

flat plan A diagram of the pages of a book used to arrange the length of chapters, the pages to be printed in colour, etc.

flexography   A form of letterpress printing that uses flexible (rubber or plastic) plates and thin inks, used mainly for printing packaging materials and also some newspapers.

flimsy   A carbon copy on very thin bank paper.

floating accent   An accent that can be set separately from the character that it usually accompanies.

flong   A form of papier mâché used for making moulds in stereotyping.

floor   The basic lower level for bids to purchase rights to publish a book in an auction.

floppy disk   A thin disk made of flexible material with one or both sides coated to accept magnetic recording. Floppy disks are usually 3½ inches, 5¼ inches, or 8 inches in diameter. Information on floppy disks can be accessed almost instantaneously as the computer scans the disk.

flush left/right   Text that is aligned vertically at the left/right margin.

flush paragraph   A paragraph in which the first word is not indented.

flyleaf   A blank leaf at the beginning or end of a book.

FOB; f o b   Abbreviation of *free on board*. This means that the supplier pays for transportation of goods to and stowage of goods on board ship or aircraft.

foil   Very thin metal, or plastic film with a silver, gold, etc., colouring, used to impress letters or a design on a book cover.

fold-out   A folded sheet in a book or magazine, which, when unfolded, opens out beyond the pages of the book. Also known as **pull-out; throw-out.**

folded and collated; folded and gathered   Used to describe folded printed but unbound sheets in order in sections of the book. Also *f and c/f and g.*

foliation   The consecutive numbering of leaves (i.e. 2 pages) of a book.

folio   (1) A sheet of paper folded in half, so making two leaves (equals four pages).   (2) A large-format book made up of such sheets.   (3) A leaf of paper in a manuscript, numbered only on the front.   (4) A page number.

follow copy   An instruction to a typesetter to set the text exactly according to the manuscript, rather than to change the text to follow the normal spelling, punctuation, etc., guidelines.

follow on   See **run on** (1).

font   (chiefly *US*) A complete assortment of types of one size and design, with all that is necessary for printing in that design. Also known as **fount.**

foolscap   See **paper sizes.**

foot   (1) The margin at the bottom of a page.   (2) The base of a piece of metal printing type.

footnote   A reference or comment at the foot of a page, at the end of a chapter, or at the end of the book.

fore-edge; foredge   The outer edge of a page, opposite the spine.

foredge margin   The margin of a page that is opposite the edge at which the pages are bound.

foreshorten   To shorten a line, form, etc., in a drawing according to perspective, in order to give an illusion of a receding form.

foreword   An introduction to a book or its author, often written by someone other than the author who is an expert on the subject.

format   (1) The size of a book or page.   (2) The general form, shape, and style of a book, including its layout, type style, paper, and binding.   (3) To arrange data or text according to specific instructions (formatting codes) that state the particular typeface size, measure, leading, etc.

forme   The type and blocks assembled in a chase and ready for printing. US equivalent: *form.*

forty-eightmo   (1) Having 48 leaves to the sheet, usually written 48mo.   (2) A book, or the size of a book, made up of such sheets.

forwarding   The set of processes in binding a book after sewing and before the cover or case is put on.

foul   (Of copy or a proof) having many errors.

fount   A complete assortment of types of one size and design, with all that is necessary for printing in that design. Also known as (especially *US*) **font.**

four-backed one, two, etc.   The printing of four colours in which sheets of paper are printed on one side in four colours and on the other side in one colour (four-backed one), two colours (four-backed two), or four colours (four-backed four).

four-colour process   A printing process using the colours cyan, magenta, yellow, and black to reproduce a complete range of colours. Colour originals are separated into films, each one representing a different colour.

fourth estate   Newspapers and journalists viewed as exercising political power, the first three 'estates' being the lords temporal (peers), the lords spiritual, and the commons.

free sheet   (1) A local newspaper or magazine that is distributed without charge. All revenue comes from advertising.   (2) (*US*) See **woodfree paper.**

freelance   A self-employed person such as a designer, photographer, or writer who pursues a profession without a long-term commitment to one employer but who is contracted to carry out particular assignments for different firms.

french fold   A single sheet of paper printed on one side only and folded without cutting the top edge so that the printed side of four pages is visible; used for greetings cards.

front-jacket flap   The part of the printed paper cover on a hardback book that folds inside the front cover.

front matter   See **prelims.**

frontispiece   An illustration facing the title-page of a book.

full binding; full bound   A hardback binding that is covered with a single piece of material. Also known as **whole bound**. See also **half binding; quarter binding.**

full-colour process   See **four-colour process.**

full out   Instruction to set a passage not indented but adjoining the margin, especially the left-hand margin.

full point   A full stop.

furniture   The pieces of wood, metal, or plastic, of various lengths and widths, put round pages of type to make margins and fasten the matter in the chase.

Gg

galley; galley proof   The first proof taken after the text has been typeset and before it is made up into pages. So called because galleys in traditional letterpress printing are the long metal trays used to hold type. Corrections are marked on galleys in red by the typesetter for the setter's errors; other corrections or changes are marked in a different colour to ensure that the cost of correcting errors is rightly apportioned.

garbage in, garbage out   A computing term meaning that the quality of information you get out is only as good as the quality of information put in, i.e. incorrect output results from incorrect input. Also *GIGO*.

gatefold   A page that is wider than the other pages and that has to be folded in on both sides. The folded parts of the page open out like a gate.

gather   To assemble the sections of a book into the correct order for binding.

gathering   A folded section of pages comprised of one sheet or part of a sheet. Also known as a **signature.**

GIGO   Abbreviation of *garbage in, garbage out*. A computing term, meaning incorrect output resulting from incorrect input.

glassine   A thin transparent or nearly transparent paper that is resistant to grease and is used for wrappings.

gloss   An explanation of an obscure or unusual word, in the margin, between the lines of a text, or as a note.

glossary   A list of terms connected with a particular subject with explanations or definitions.

gm²   Abbreviation of *grams per square metre,* a metric method of measuring the substance of paper. Also known as **g/m²; gsm.**

gold   Used for stamping designs on a book cover, in leaf form (foil).

goldenrod   (chiefly *US*) An opaque yellow or orange masking paper used in preparing flats.

golfball   The popular description of the spherical typehead found on the IBM electric typewriter. The print element is shaped like a golfball and the letters and symbols are embossed on the outside of the 'ball', which can be changed for different designs, typesizes, etc.

Gothic   (1) A form of type with a heavy face and elaborate angular features, commonly thought of as 'Old English' script. Also known as **black letter.**   (2) A square-cut type without serifs.

grain   The direction or pattern of the fibres of a manufactured sheet of paper. Pages of a book tend to open more easily if the grain direction is parallel to the spine, but printers generally prefer the grain to cross the printing direction to avoid stretching or shrinking in changing moisture conditions.

grammage   The metric method of measuring the substance of paper in grams per square metre. See **gm².**

graphic   Relating to writing, drawing, engraving, or graphics.

graphic arts   The visual arts concerned with representation, illustration, typography, printing, etc., on a flat surface and the methods associated with these techniques.

graphics   (1) Designs containing typography and illustrations.   (2) See **graphic arts.**   (3) The information displayed as pictures or diagrams on a VDU as a result of data processing.

grave   The accent `. See also **accent.**

gravure An intaglio printing process in which an image is etched or sunk below the surface of a copper printing plate or cylinder. The recesses that are so made are filled with ink, and as the paper is fed through the press, it is pressed into the recesses to pick up the ink, which is transferred onto the paper.

grey board Best-quality board made from a solid fibre-sheet, used in binding.

grid A guide used by designers to ensure consistent design for a particular book or series of books, showing trim sizes, column depths, type widths, text and illustration areas, etc.

grippers (In printing presses) the metal fingers that hold the sheet of paper in the correct position and control its flow as it passes through the press.

ground (In etching) a thin layer of resinous substance that is impervious to acid and so protects the parts of a plate that do not bear the image.

groundwood (*US*) Mechanically ground wood pulp. See **mechanical.**

gsm Abbreviation of *grams per square metre,* a metric method of measuring the substance of paper. See **gm²**.

guillemets The quotation marks « » used in French and in some other foreign-language publications.

guillotine A device for cutting paper and card.

gutter (1) The space between imposed pages in a forme. (2) The blank space between two facing pages of a book.

Hh

H & J See **hyphenation and justification.**

hache Symbol # used to mean 'number', and in proof-reading and marking up copy to refer to a space.

hair space A space of one-twelfth of a set em.

half binding; half bound A hardback binding in which the back (spine) and corners are covered with one material, the sides with a different material.

half-title The first printed page of a book, a right-hand page, containing only the title and preceding the title-page. Also known as **bastard title.**

half-tone A photographic process which represents light and shade by dots of equal density but different sizes, the image being photographed through a screen.

half-tone screen A sheet of glass or film that has a grid, used in the half-tone photographic process to divide an image into dots. The fineness of the screen is represented in lines per inch or lines per centimetre. For example a 133 screen (per inch) is 54 screen (per centimetre).

half up An illustration that is drawn 1½ times the size at which it will finally appear.

hanging indentation Describing the first line of a paragraph which is printed full out left, with the next lines indented. Also known as **reverse indent.**

hard copy Permanent output from a computer; printed matter, in contrast to copy electronically stored or displayed (soft copy).

hard hyphen   In word processing and computer type-setting, a hyphen that is an integral part of the word. A hard hyphen is always retained wherever the word appears in the line.

hardback   A book with stiff board covers. US equivalent: *hardcover.*

head   The top edge of a page.

head margin   The space that is between the printed area and the top of the page.

headband   A narrow decorative cord of cotton or silk glued to the top of the spine of a cased book.

heading   A title of a chapter, division, or subdivision of printed matter.

headline   The line at the top of a page containing the title of the book or a chapter title.

headword   A word that begins a paragraph, a chapter, or an entry in a reference book such as a dictionary.

heat-transfer copier   A small desktop copier which operates on a principle of extreme heat, from an infra-red light source. The original with the copy paper on top is exposed to the heat and where the print occurs on the original the heat is intensified to 'burn' a black facsimile of the original on to the copy paper. The paper continues to be sensitive to heat even after copying. This machine can produce ink stencil and spirit duplicating masters, overhead transparencies and can laminate paper and card.

hectograph carbon   Special carbon paper used to prepare masters for use on the spirit duplicator. It comes in different colours, especially purple, blue, red, or green.

height-to-paper   The standard overall height of letter-press type, 0.918 in (23.3 mm).

hickey   (In offset lithography) a printing defect caused by a speck of dirt on the plate or blanket cylinder.

highlight   The lightest part of a photographic half-tone reproduction.

horizontal format   (*US*) See **landscape.**

hot-metal typesetting   Used to describe machines or methods using type made from molten metal.

house corrections   Corrections to proofs made by the publisher, typesetter, or printer, in contrast to those made by the author.

house style   The set of guidelines on spelling, punctuation, and linguistic usage of a printer, typesetter, or publisher, to ensure consistency of style in the material produced.

hype   Exaggerated publicity for a product.

hyphenate   To use a hyphen to divide a word, syllable, etc.

hyphenation and justification (In computerised typesetting) the set of instructions for hyphenating words at the end of lines and for distributing spaces in the correct places in lines of type, according to the justification required.

ibid Abbreviation for *ibidem*, a Latin word meaning 'in the same place', used in a reference note or bibliography to refer to the same book, chapter, etc., as previously mentioned.

idem A Latin word meaning 'the same', used in a reference note or bibliography to refer to an article, book, author, etc., previously mentioned.

illustration (1) A drawing, photograph, painting, etc., used to explain or decorate a text. (2) A picture that is drawn in contrast to a photograph.

image area (In lithographic printing) the area to be printed, which accepts ink but repels water. The non-image area, in contrast, accepts water and rejects ink, so that when ink and water are applied to the whole surface, only the image area is printed.

image printer Using optical technology, a printer which will compose an image of a complete page from digital input, final copy being produced as print on paper.

impact printing A means of printing where the characters are formed on the paper by means of a hammer striking the ribbon, e.g. dot-matrix printers and line printers.

imperial See **paper sizes.**

imposition The assembling of pages prior to printing so that they will be in the right order when the sheet is folded. To *impose* is to assemble pages in this way.

impression (1) A single printing of a book. A reprint having only minor corrections is a new impression. (2) The bringing into contact of a printing surface and the paper, etc., being printed.

impression cylinder The cylinder on a printing press that brings the paper, etc., being printed into contact with the inked printing plate, cylinder, etc. (the blanket cylinder in offset printing).

imprimatur The official licence to print a book, etc.

imprint The name and address of the publisher and the printer, and the date and place of publication of a book. The publisher's imprint appears on the title-page, the printer's on the verso or on the last page of a book.

imprint page The reverse of the title-page with details of the printer, publisher, the copyright notice, ISBN, etc.

in house Of work undertaken within an organisation or company such as a publisher, not bought in from an outside individual or company.

in print Available from the publisher.

indent Instruction to a typesetter to begin a line with a blank space.

indentation The blank space at the beginning of a line printed further in from the margin than subsequent lines.

index (1) An alphabetical list of subjects, names, etc., dealt with, usually at the end of a book, with page references. (2) See **fist.**

indexer A person who specialises in compiling indexes for an author or publisher.

India paper A thin strong opaque paper, used for printing Bibles and dictionaries.

indirect costs Costs such as rent, administration, and other overheads that are not directly related to a particular task, in contrast to *direct costs*.

indirect process Refers to the method of photocopying, as in plain-paper copiers, where a photoconductive coating is formed of the original document inside the photocopying unit. This image is then transferred to an ordinary sheet of paper which undergoes a heating process to make it into a permanent copy.

inferior   Of a small letter or number set below the line (the base line), e.g. the number 2 in H_2O.

initial   The initial letter of a chapter set as a large capital and extending over two or three lines at the beginning of the chapter.

initial caps   Instruction to a typesetter to set the first letter of a word as a capital.

ink duplicator   Sometimes referred to as a *stencil duplicator*, a machine which can give 5000 or more good copies from a single master stencil which has been prepared by hand, typewriter, electronic stencil cutter or thermal photocopier.

ink-jet printer   A printer controlled by digitally stored information whose main feature is that each copy can differ, as the printing is individually controlled. Each character is generated by a drop of liquid which is vibrated, a charge passed through it and then deflected by electrostatic fields. The deflection is varied so that the ink drops are directed to specific parts of the paper sheet.

inking roller   A roller in a printing press that transfers ink from the ink supply to the printing plate or plate cylinder.

input device   A piece of equipment which allows data and instructions to be entered into a computer's memory, e.g. keyboard, terminal, light pen, OCR.

insert   Printed matter such as a bookmark or advertisement placed in a book and not secured in any way.

inset   (1) A printed section of at least four pages placed inside another section, usually at the centre of another section, before binding.   (2) A small illustration, such as a map, set within a larger one.

inspection copy A copy of a book sent to a lecturer, teacher, etc., for his or her recommendation to students. The copy must be returned or paid for, or may be retained free of charge if a certain number of additional copies of the book are ordered.

intaglio A printing process in which the image on a plate, or cylinder is sunk below the surface, as in the gravure process.

interactive Of a system that immediately responds to input in a continuous user/system dialogue. It allows a two-way communication between the user and the computer, i.e. information/data can be keyed in and information can be requested.

interface The boundary or connecting device between two different pieces of computer equipment which are not compatible. Such a device could be used to enable a word processor to 'communicate' with a phototypesetter.

interleaf (plural *interleaves*) A blank additional leaf inserted between the regular leaves of a printed text, for reference notes or to protect an illustration. To *interleave* is to introduce interleaves into a book.

interlinear Material set in a small type size between larger lines of type, e.g. a New Testament in Greek with an English translation set between the lines of the Greek.

Intertype® A kind of composing machine that casts complete lines of type; also a kind of computerised photosetting system.

intro Abbreviation of *introduction*, especially the opening paragraph of a text.

introduction A preliminary part of a book, written by the author or by an expert writing about the subject.

inverted commas The single (' ') or double (" ") punctuation marks used to show the beginning and end of a quotation. See also **quotation marks.**

ISBN Abbreviation of *International Standard Book Number*, a ten-digit number that identifies each separate publication, including a new edition of a book. The ISBN is divided into four parts. The first part shows the language area in which a book is published (e.g. 0 and 1 for the English language area). The second part shows the specific publisher, the third part shows one title or edition of that title, and finally comes a check digit. The ISBN is often also included in the bar code on the back of a book.

ISSN Abbreviation of *International Standard Serial Number*, a similar system to the ISBN used for magazines and periodicals. The eight-digit number shows the countries of the journal's publication and its title.

ital Abbreviation of **italic.**

italic The type that slopes to the right, either using specially designed characters (*true italic*) or, in computerised typesetting, created electronically from roman characters (*sloped roman*). Italic is used for emphasis in the text and is shown on a manuscript, galley proof, etc., by a single underlining.

Jj

jacket The removable paper cover of a book. Also known as **dust cover; dust jacket; wrapper.**

jobbing Miscellaneous printing work, especially of business cards, stationery, letterheads, rather than books.

joint venture A business activity undertaken by two or more companies acting together, sharing the costs, risks, and profits.

journal A periodical concerned with specialist subjects; a daily newspaper.

justification The adjusting of the positions of words on a page, distributing additional space in lines so that the right margin forms a straight vertical and parallel edge to the left margin. See also **hyphenation and justification.**

justified text Text which has an even right margin equal to the left margin and where the right-hand margin appears vertically straight.

justify To adjust the positions of words on a page, distributing additional space in lines so that the right margin forms a straight vertical and parallel edge to the left margin.

Kk

keep standing An instruction to keep type, film, or plates in page form after the first printing, in preparation for possible reprints.

kern The part of a type that projects beyond the body and rests on an adjoining letter.

kerning The deliberate reduction of space between two characters, particularly in large display type, so that they appear closer together.

key (1) A button on a keyboard which is depressed or touched to register a character.   (2) To enter text on a keyboard into a computerised typesetting system.

keyboard (1) An input device for a computer, usually alphanumeric but also containing special keys which perform particular functions and which is manually operated to input data or instructions.   (2) To *keyboard* is to type in the copy into a computerised typesetting system.

keyline The outline drawing on artwork that shows the shape, size, or position for an illustration, half-tone, tint, etc., sometimes itself reproduced.

keystroke The single act of pressing down a key on a keyboard device.

keyword A significant word, as of the title of a book, that is used to retrieve information from a computerised data system.

kiss impression An extremely light printing impression that produces an image on paper.

kraft Very strong brown paper, made from unbleached wood pulp.

Kurzweil Data Entry Machine   A device that 'learns' to read any typeface and then, with the aid of an operator, transforms printed or typewritten texts directly into electronic form, so avoiding the need for the text to be keyed (typed) again. See also **optical character recognition.**

KWIC/KWOC   Abbreviation of *key word in/out of context*, an index that has been generated by a computer. In KWIC, the keywords, showing part of their contexts, are listed in alphabetical order. In KWOC, the context is preceded by the keyword.

Ll

lacquer A clear coating that is applied to give a glossy finish to a printed sheet.

laid paper Paper that has a pattern of watermarked parallel lines (*laid lines*), from the wire marks of a mould or the dandy roll in a papermaking machine.

lamination The thin transparent glossy plastic coating that covers a book jacket, certificate, menu, etc., to protect it, applied by heat and pressure.

landscape A book or illustration having the longer sides at head and foot. Contrast with *portrait*. US equivalent: *horizontal format*.

large crown See **book sizes**.

large print Of books printed in a very large type, for reading by the partially sighted. Large-print books are often sold direct to libraries.

laser An acronym for *l*ight *a*mplification by the *s*imulated *e*mission of *r*adiation. A device emitting a powerful pure light producing a narrow light beam which can be used for a range of communication activities, e.g. printing and optical scanning.

laser disk A form of video used to access information held on disk rather than on tape. The disk is read by decoding patterns produced by a laser light reflected off the disk's surface.

laser printer A printer using a laser light source to write on paper which is then passed through an ink powder. Ink is attracted to the area on the paper which has been written on and excess powder is removed. The ink is then fixed by chemical treatment or heat. Laser printers give high-quality output at speeds of eight pages a minute upwards, operate very quietly, and have the additional facility to be able to print form headings at the same time as information, so that pre-printed stationery is not required.

launch   The introduction, especially with great publicity and a special presentation, of a new book, magazine, etc., onto the market.

layout   A plan of a job showing position of type, illustrations, and specifying typesizes and typefaces.

lc   Abbreviation of **lower case.**

lead   The main news story in a newspaper.

leader   A row of dots used to guide the eye across the page.

leading   Additional spacing between lines of type, originally made with strips of lead.

leaf   A single piece of paper; two pages.

leaflet   A single folded sheet of paper, used especially for advertising purposes.

legend   The descriptive heading or accompanying wording of an illustration.

lemma   A headword at the start of a textual note.

Letraset®   A kind of transfer lettering.

letterhead   The official (heading on) notepaper of an organisation which includes the firm's logo (trademark), the name, address and telephone number, telex code number, fax number, and information legally required such as registered office address (if a company), registration number, and VAT number.

letterpress   (1) The printing process from raised type or blocks, the printing surface being inked by rollers, and then impressed against the paper.   (2) The text of a book, in contrast to illustrations.

letterset   A printing method in which ink is transferred from a raised surface onto a blanket and then offset onto the paper. The method does not use water. Also known as **dry offset.**

letterspacing   Adding small spaces between characters, usually capitals or small capitals, to enhance the appearance of a line. Letterspacing is shown by inserting short vertical lines between letters.

libel   A written accusation; a malicious defamatory publication or statement.

library binding   The strengthened binding for paperbacks or hardbacks on books for libraries.

ligature   A type of two or more letters joined together as a single unit, e.g. fl, fi.

light box   A box that has a semi-transparent lid which is illuminated from beneath, that enables colour transparencies, prints, etc., to be checked.

light face   The relatively thin light form of a typeface. Contrast with *bold face.*

light pen   A device which looks like a pen but has a light-sensitive tip, which is used for reading bar codes. The light pen is moved across the bar code and it interprets the light and dark strips for direct input to the computer. The same device can be used by designers who 'draw' diagrams/lines on the VDU with the tip of the pen, the computer then converts the diagram to data for storage.

limited edition   An edition of a book that is restricted to a particular number of copies, sometimes numbered individually and signed by the author.

limp   (Of a binding) not stiff or rigid with boards, especially having a flexible cover made of artificial cloth.

line and half-tone   Of a process that combines line artwork and half-tones.

line artwork Drawings, diagrams, etc., that consist solely of black lines on white and tint areas, with no intermediate tones and so not needing to be reproduced as half-tones.

line block A relief block prepared from line artwork, for letterpress printing.

line conversion The process, by photographic or electronic means, of changing half-tones or continuous tones into ordinary black-on-white artwork, by eliminating middle tones.

line feed The distance, measured in points, millimetres, or inches, between the base lines of successive lines of text.

line gauge (*US*) A ruler marked with points, picas, etc., to measure type widths, the depth of a page, etc.

line length The number of characters printed horizontally across one line of a page between the left- and right-hand margins.

line printer A device for printing computer output producing text one line at a time. Sets of characters on continuous belts are contained within the printer. As paper is fed past the printing head, an entire line of characters is printed.

line spacing The number of lines of space which appear between each typed line of text and added to the line of text for counting purposes, e.g. single line spacing is one line of text with no space between it and the next line of text. Double line spacing is one line of text with one line of space before the next line of text.

lining figures Arabic numbers that are of equal height, aligning at the top and bottom: 1234567890. Contrast with *non-lining figures*.

linocut A design cut in relief in linoleum; a print made from such a block.

Linotype® A make of typesetting equipment. The original Linotype machine was operated by a keyboard and produced a complete line of type on one solid metal slug.

Linson® A kind of strong paper used instead of book cloth in binding.

list The set of titles that a publisher has available for sale.

literal A wrong letter in printed or typed matter resulting from a mistake made by the typesetter. Also known as **typo.**

literary agent See **agent** (1).

lithography A printing process that uses the principle that water and grease (ink) do not mix. Printing from a flat-image surface, plates are prepared so that the non-printing area attracts water and rejects ink, whereas the printing area accepts ink and rejects water. See also **offset lithography.**

loc cit Abbreviation for *loco citato*, a Latin phrase meaning 'in the place cited', used as a reference in notes.

lock up To secure the printing type, blocks, etc., in a chase (metal frame) or on the bed of a printing machine by tightening the quoins.

logotype (1) Several letters or a word that are cast as one item. (2) The identifying symbol, design, trademark, etc., of a company or organisation.

long descenders The descenders on the characters of a typeface that are longer in comparison with the normal design of that typeface.

long page A page that has one or two extra lines to avoid an unsightly break.

loose-leaf Having a binding with two or more rings that may be opened to allow perforated sheets of paper to be easily inserted or removed.

lower case The small letters of the alphabet. See also **case** (2).

Mm

machine composition (Hot-metal) typesetting using machines operated by a keyboard.

machine direction The direction of the grain of paper in a papermaking machine.

machine-finished Of paper that has been finished on a papermaking machine. Also *MF*. See also **calender.**

machine-glazed Of paper that is made on a special machine with a drying cylinder that gives a high glaze to one side of the paper only, for example wrapping paper. Also *MG*.

machine proof A proof taken on the printing machine, offering the last chance to correct errors before printing.

machine-readable Of data that can be read by a machine, such as an optical character reader, without the text needing to be keyed in manually.

machine-readable code A bar code in the form of vertical lines used on packaging and book covers to identify and contain information about a product. Bar codes can be read by a wand, light pen or bar-code scanner. A supplementary code may be added to show the price of an article. See also **bar code; ISBN.**

macron The straight mark ⁻ used to indicate a long vowel or syllable.

magazine A publication issued regularly containing articles, stories, etc., by various people, usually including advertisements.

magnetic-ink character recognition Numbers printed in magnetic ink which can be read visually and by a computer's MICR reader, e.g. numbers which are printed across the bottom of bank cheques. Also *MICR*.

magnification   The process of making a photograph, illustration, etc., larger in reproduction; the amount by which the photograph, etc., is made larger.

mailshot   The sending by post of information, advertising a product to possible customers.

majuscule   A capital letter.

make-up   The arrangement of composed type into columns or pages, including the insertion of illustrative matter, captions, headlines, notes, etc.

makeover   (*US*) The inevitable wastage of materials in the printing process.

makeready   The preparation and adjustment of a printing press before the printing begins, including setting the press to accept the paper, checking the ink and colours.

making   An order for special size, quantity, or colour of paper.

manila; manilla   A strong usually brown or buff paper, used especially for envelopes.

manuscript   The text of a book, etc., written or typed, that is submitted for publication. Also *MS*.

marbling   The decorative colouring of the endpapers of books or book edges to resemble marble.

margin   The space on a printed page that surrounds the printed text.

mark up   (1) To prepare a manuscript for typesetting by specifying typographical instructions. (2) To set a higher price, the *mark-up* being the increase on the cost price of goods for sale to allow for the seller's profit.

marked proof   The proof on which corrections and queries have been marked by a printer's reader.

marketing department   The section within an organisation that has responsibility for carrying out activities such as market research, advertising, public relations or customer relations, and sales and after-sales service.

mask   To cover the areas on the edge of a photograph which are not to be reproduced.

master proof   A proof that has been read and marked with corrections.

masthead   The name of a newspaper or periodical in the typographical form in which it normally appears; a similar block of information regularly used as a heading.

matrix   (plural *matrices*) (1) (In hot-metal composition) a mould used for casting type.   (2) (In phototypesetting) the photographic negative of a character, from which the image is produced.   (3) (In stereotyping) the mould or mat taken from original relief printing material.

matrix printer   See **dot-matrix printer.**

matter   Material to be printed or type that has been set.

measure   The width of a column or page of type, usually expressed in 12 point (or pica) ems.

mechanical   (1) (Of paper) containing a large amount of mechanical ground wood pulp but also some chemical pulp, used especially in newsprint.   (2) Camera-ready artwork including typeset text, photographs, etc., in position.

mechanical binding   Binding by means of a special device such as a tightly fitting plastic gripper, or a plastic or wire coil inserted through holes in the paper, the latter device being useful where it is important that the book lies flat. In **spiral binding** the pages and cover are joined by a wire or plastic spiral coil. In **wire binding** a metal device with looping finger-like parts is slotted through the punched papers and cover. **(Plastic-)comb binding** is the equivalent in plastic.

mechanical tint   A pattern of dots or lines or a solid panel in a second colour, which can be laid down on artwork and reproduced as line artwork.

medium   (1) Any material used to store information, e.g. magnetic disk, magnetic tape. The word is often used in the plural, *media*.   (2) The weight of a typeface, between light and bold.   (3) See **paper sizes.**

memoirs   (1) A collection of personal reminiscences. (2) The record of the transactions of a society.

memory   A device in the central processing unit of a computer which can store information for extraction by the computer when required. Memory is measured in bytes with each byte representing one character, letter, number, symbol, etc. The amount of memory is an indication of the computer's power; the larger the memory, the greater the power.

menu   A list of possible options or facilities presented to the user from data or word processing software on a computer. Choice is normally displayed on the VDU of a terminal and selection is made via the keyboard.

merge   To combine information from two or more sources, e.g. address lists or mailing lists with document files or form letters.

micro   A microcomputer and a category for the smallest computers which use a microprocessor as its processing element.

microcomputer   A category for the smallest computers which uses a microprocessor as its processing element, having sufficient peripherals and memory to link with the outside world and store information. The smallest forms of micro consist of a VDU with keyboard, screen display, and microprocessor which acts as a central processing unit.

microfiche   A form of microfilm where pages of text are photographically reduced and mounted onto a frame (as in a negative). Microfiche can be read a frame at a time using a microfiche reader, a special optical device which will illuminate frames of fiche and provide an enlarged image which can be projected onto a screen to be read by the user.

microfilm   A type of microform in which pages of text are photographically reduced in sequence onto a roll of film. Microfilm is often used as a filing process which is developed to copy all kinds of material in reduced form for storing e.g. newspapers on microfilm. Microfilm is read by means of a special optical device which will magnify each page and present the image in an enlarged form on a screen which can then be read by the user.

microform   An extremely small photographic reproduction such as microfiche and microfilm.

microprocessor   Sometimes a synonym for microcomputer, but more correctly the central processor in which all elements of a control unit are contained on a single chip.

millboard   A hard strong good-quality board, traditionally made from rope, and used for book covers.

minicomputer   A medium sized computer, smaller than mainframe but larger than micro with either general or specialised usage including process control, often used by a medium sized company to keep records, payroll, stock, etc.

mint   (Of a book, etc) in perfect condition, as if unused.

minuscule   A lower-case letter.

miscellany   A collection of writings on different subjects or by different authors.

misprint   A mistake in printing.

mixing   The combining of different designs and sizes of typefaces.

mock-up   A rough presentation of a printed text, package, etc., showing size, colours, etc.

modem   An acronym formed from the words *mod*ulator/*dem*odulator. A device for converting a digital signal from a computer into an analogue signal which can then be transmitted along a standard telephone line. The received signal can be reconverted from analogue to digital by the same device at the receiving end.

modern numerals   Arabic numbers that are of equal height, aligning at the top and bottom: 123, etc. Also known as **lining figures.**

modern typefaces   Typefaces marked by a great contrast between thick and thin strokes and fine squared off serifs.

moiré   The undesirable watered-silk pattern that occurs when screens are set at the wrong angles in reproduction.

mold   (*US*) See **mould.**

monochrome   A single colour with varying tones.

monogram   A design formed by several letters, especially initials, interwoven as one.

monograph   A scholarly book, paper, etc., written on a particular subject.

Monophoto®   A kind of computer-driven photographic composition system.

monospacing   Letters typed all of the same set and width as on a standard typewriter. Compare with *proportional spacing.*

Monotype®   A make of typesetting equipment. The original Monotype machine cast and set type letter by letter in hot metal; a reproduction made by this process.

montage   The combination of several separate drawings or photographs to make a single composite design.

morocco   A kind of fine-leather goatskin used in binding books.

mottling   A spotty uneven printing appearance.

mould   (In hot-metal composition) the part in which the type body is cast. US spelling: *mold.*

mouse   A device which can be rolled across the surface of a graphics table. When a button on the mouse is depressed, the computer will address the item in the mouse position.

movable type   (In older typesetting methods) the casting of individual pieces of metal each bearing a particular letter of the alphabet and fitting these into lines with metal spaces.

MS   (plural *MSS*) Abbreviation of **manuscript.**

multi-ring binder   A form of mechanical binding in which a number of rings placed near one another keep the pages of a book secure.

multiplexing   The use of a single telecommunications link to transmit a number of different signals either simultaneously or in rapid succession.

mutton   See **em** (1).

Nn

narrow measure Type that is set in narrow widths, usually in columns.

NCR Abbreviation of *no carbon required,* chemically impregnated paper which produces an image on second and subsequent sheets of paper upon impact.

nd Abbreviation of *no date*, used in bibliographies where a book does not show its date of publication.

NE Abbreviation of *new edition*, response by a publisher to a bookseller when a new edition is in preparation.

negative Photographic film that has been previously exposed and developed to show a reversal of tones and lines in black-and-white photography.

NEP Abbreviation of *new edition in preparation*, response by a publisher to a bookseller.

net With no discount allowed. See also **net book.**

net book A book with a fixed price. Net books, under the Net Book Agreement, may not be sold at less than the price fixed by the publisher.

net receipts The amount received by a publisher for the sale of books after deducting discounts and commissions.

news agency An organisation that collects news and for a payment sells the reports to newspapers, periodicals, and television and radio companies.

newspaper A publication issued usually daily or weekly containing news, reviews, features, and advertisements.

newsprint Paper made mainly from mechanical wood pulp and used for printing newspapers.

NK Abbreviation of *not known,* a response by a publisher to a bookseller to an order for a book that is not their publication.

nl Abbreviation for *new line*, an instruction to a typesetter to set the text on a new line.

non-fiction The class of literature consisting of books dealing with facts, etc., rather than imaginary stories.

non-image area (In lithographic printing) the area that is not to be printed which accepts water and rejects ink. The image area, in contrast, accepts ink and rejects water, so that when ink and water are applied to the whole surface, only the image area is printed.

non-impact printing Printers which do not require physical impact for printing characters on paper, e.g. ink-jet printing and electrostatic printing. Contrast with *impact printing*.

non-lining figures Arabic numbers that have ascenders and descenders: 1234567890 . Contrast with *lining figures*. Also known as **non-ranging figures.**

non-net book A book that a bookseller may sell at less than the price fixed by the publisher. Non-net books are sometimes marked with an asterisk * after the price.

non-ranging figures See **non-lining figures.**

notch binding A technique in perfect binding in which notches are cut into the spine of a section and glue penetrates into the perforations to join the sections together.

novel A fairly long fictitious story.

np Abbreviation for *new paragraph*, an instruction to a typesetter to set the text as a (usually indented) new paragraph.

nut See **en.**

NYP Abbreviation of *not yet published*, a response by a publisher to a bookseller to an order for a book that is not yet available.

Oo

obelisk   The character † used as a (second-level) reference mark, especially to a footnote. Also known as **dagger.**

oblique   The stroke /. See **solidus.**

oblong   A book that has the longer sides at the head and foot. Also known as **landscape.**

OCR   Abbreviation of *optical character recognition*. Characters printed on a document in a way that can be read both by an observer and by computer OCR readers.

octavo   (1) Having eight leaves to the sheet, usually written 8vo.   (2) A book, or the size of a book, made up of such sheets.

odd pages   The right-hand (recto) pages, i.e. those with odd numbers.

oddment   Part of a book that has to be printed separately when the text does not fit into (usually 32-page) sheets: see **even working.**

off-line   A terminal or other computer component not connected to or controlled by a central processing unit. Contrast with *on-line*.

offcut   A remnant of a piece of paper cut from a larger piece.

offprint   A printing of a single article from a periodical. Also known as **separate.**

offset lithography   The most common form of photo-lithography, the process of lithographic printing from a photographically prepared plate using greasy ink. The image is transferred (offset) onto a rubber-covered cylinder (the blanket cylinder) and then to the paper, board, etc. See also **lithography.**

Old English   See **Gothic** (1).

old face   Of a typeface marked by a strong triangular serif, little contrast between light and heavy strokes, and diagonal curved strokes. Also known as **old style.**

old-style numerals   Arabic numbers that have ascenders or descenders: 1234567890.

omnibus   Of a book containing reprints of several works, especially ones by a single author or on a single subject.

on-line   A terminal or other component directly connected to the central processing unit in a computer system and which will interact directly with the central processor. Contrast with *off-line.*

one-shot rights   The right to publish a complete book or an abridgment of it in one issue of a periodical or newspaper, in contrast to a serialised reprint.

onion skin   A very thin glazed translucent paper.

OO   Abbreviation of *on order*, a response by a publisher to a bookseller, showing that the book is being ordered, especially from the printer's or binder's warehouse.

OP   Abbreviation of *out of print*, a response by a publisher to a bookseller to an order for an individual book that is no longer available from the publisher.

op cit   Abbreviation of *opera citato*, a Latin phrase meaning 'in the work cited', used with the author's name to refer to the same book as quoted in a previous reference.

opacity   The quality of non-transparency of printing paper.

open-flat   Of books for which it is important that the pages lie flat when the book is opened. See **mechanical binding.**

open market Equal unrestricted selling opportunities of different editions of the same book in particular countries agreed by different publishers.

opening A pair of facing pages in a book.

optical centring The positioning of text, especially a title or poetry, so that it appears to be centrally positioned, although it is in fact not.

optical character reader A machine which reads printed letters, numbers, or symbols and compares them with those stored in its memory generating that letter, number, or symbol in a computer readable form.

optical character recognition A technique in which information in the form of characters, numbers, or symbols is read by an optical scanning device, or optical character reader, which converts the information into computer readable form. Also known as **OCR.**

option clause The section in a contract between a publisher and author that the author shall offer his or her next work or works to that same publisher.

original Any text or illustration that is to be used for photographic reproduction.

origination The series of operations to prepare text and illustrations for printing, including editorial work, typesetting, and the preparation of illustrations.

orphan The unsightly first line of a paragraph that appears at the foot of a page.

OS Abbreviation of *out of stock*, reply from a publisher to a bookseller that copies of a book are not immediately available, because a new printing, shipment, etc., is awaited.

out The inadvertent omission of material in typesetting.

out of print No longer available from the publisher, and since the publisher has no intention to reprint, the title is discontinued.

output device   A device capable of receiving information from a central processor or peripheral unit which translates computer information into another medium, e.g. a VDU or printer.

outwork   Work, such as design or editing, commissioned by a publisher and undertaken off the publisher's premises.

overexpose   To expose a film, plate, etc., to too much light.

overhead projector   A visual method of presenting data by the use of a transparency which has been prepared either by writing, drawing, or typing directly onto acetate sheets called overhead projector transparencies, or by photocopying onto transparencies from documents or diagrams using a thermal copier. The transparency is placed onto an overhead projector and the image is magnified and displayed above the projector so that it can be seen by a group of people.

overheads   Costs that cannot be measured directly as part of the cost of producing a particular product. Examples of overheads are office staff salaries, rent, insurance, heating, and lighting.

overlay   (1) A transparent sheet over artwork, on which instructions are written.   (2) A transparent sheet used in presenting line artwork for colour reproduction, each colour being drawn in black on an overlay.

overmatter   Text that has been typeset but cannot be printed because of shortage of space. Also known as **overset.**

overprint   To print over already printed matter.

overrunning   Rearranging lines of type within a paragraph when a correction makes a line shorter or longer, achieved by moving words from one line to another and altering the spacing between them.

overs   Paper supplied beyond the ordered number to compensate for sheets spoilt during production.

overstocks   More stock at a bookshop or publisher than is needed to supply customers' orders.

Ozalid®   A method of proofing film-set matter onto chemically treated paper; a reproduction made by this process. Also known as **blueprints; blues; Vandykes.**

Pp

packager A company that conceives, commissions, designs, and produces illustrated books that are sold to a publisher as finished products.

page One side of a leaf of paper.

page make-up The arrangement of composed type into pages including the insertion of illustrative matter, captions, headlines, notes, etc.

page proofs Proofs of pages which have not been imposed.

pages to view The number of pages that are printed on one side of a sheet.

pagination The numbering of pages in a book, periodical, etc. The preliminary pages of a longer book are often numbered using Roman numerals, while the text pages are numbered using Arabic numerals.

pamphlet A short unbound publication usually with a soft cover.

Pantone Matching System® A reference system for inks, films, papers, marker pens, etc., in which different colours on swatches are numbered and can be checked and mixed accordingly by a printer.

paper Substance made of cellulose fibres, e.g. of wood and cloth, mixed with other additives and formed into thin flat sheets.

paper sizes Traditional paper sizes, untrimmed, are:

crown	15 in × 20 in	381 mm × 508 mm
demy	17½ in × 22½ in	445 mm × 572 mm
foolscap	13½ in × 17 in	343 mm × 432 mm

imperial	22 in × 30 in	559 mm × 762 mm
medium	18 in × 23 in	457 mm × 584 mm
royal	20 in × 25 in	508 mm × 635 mm

Metric, A sizes, trimmed are:

A0	841 mm × 1189 mm
A1	594 mm × 841 mm
A2	420 mm × 594 mm
A3	297 mm × 420 mm
A4	210 mm × 297 mm
A5	148 mm × 210 mm
A6	105 mm × 148 mm
A7	74 mm × 105 mm
A8	52 mm × 74 mm
A9	37 mm × 52 mm
A10	26 mm × 37 mm

Traditional US paper sizes, untrimmed, are:

16 in × 21 in	26 in × 40 in
17 in × 22 in	26 in × 48 in
17 in × 28 in	28 in × 34 in
19 in × 24 in	28 in × 42 in
20 in × 26 in	28 in × 44 in
21 in × 32 in	32 in × 44 in
22 in × 24 in	34 in × 44 in
22 in × 34 in	35 in × 45 in
22½ in × 35 in	35 in × 46 in
23 in × 35 in	36 in × 48 in
24 in × 36 in	38 in × 50 in
24 in × 38 in	38 in × 52 in
25 in × 38 in	41 in × 54 in
26 in × 34 in	44 in × 64 in

paperback A book with a flexible paper cover, normally one with a perfect binding.

paragraph mark The mark ¶ used to show a new paragraph or as a reference mark.

parallel folding The folding of paper in which each fold is parallel to the other, for example in concertina folding.

parchment The skin of a sheep, goat, or other animal treated, and used for writing on; strong paper designed to imitate animal parchment, especially a high-quality bond or cream wove writing paper.

parentheses The pair of characters ( ) used to mark off a supplementary or explanatory word or passage in a sentence, to enclose letters or numbers in a series, and in mathematical or logical expressions. Also known as **round brackets.**

part work A series of magazines published regularly that are designed to be bound together to form a complete book.

pass (1) A single complete operation of a printing press or phototypesetting system. (2) An instruction to undertake printing, after all the corrections have been made.

paste-up (1) A layout in which galley proofs are pasted down to pages and outlines are drawn to show the rough size and position of illustrations. (2) Text pasted up as finished artwork, ready for reproduction. US equivalent: *mechanical.*

pasteboard Stiff board made of sheets of paper pasted together, used in bookbinding.

pastel Substance made of ground pigment mixed with gum, in the form of sticks and used for drawing.

patch A set of corrected lines or paragraphs in phototypesetting.

PC Abbreviation of *personal computer*, a microcomputer suitable for use in the home.

PE Abbreviation of *printer's error*, an error that is the fault of the typesetter, not the author or publisher.

perfect binding   An unsewn book binding in which the backs of the gathered sections are sheared off and the leaves held in place by glue, used particularly for paperbacks. Also known as **adhesive binding; unsewn binding.**

perfecting   Printing on the second side of a sheet of paper when the first side has already been printed. Also known as **backing-up.**

perfector   A printing press that prints both sides of a sheet in a single operation.

perforate   To make rows of small holes or slots in paper or board, especially so that different parts may be separated from each other.

period   (*US*) A full stop.

periodical   A magazine or journal issued regularly, for example monthly or quarterly.

peripheral units   Additional facilities which can be added to a computer configuration for special applications. Some examples are: letter quality printers, telex pad, optical character recognition, robots and fax machines.

permission   Permission that needs to be obtained before copyright material can be reproduced.

photocomposition   See **phototypesetting.**

photocopier   A machine which will reproduce an exact copy of an original document through the action of heat, electrostatic charge or light. Accurate copies are produced without the need for a skilled operator. Drawings, graphs, and even photographs in some cases can be copied direct from an original document.

photoengraving   A method of making relief printing plates for a line or half-tone illustration, in which an image (the half-tone being screened) is photographed on a plate and then etched by having the unsensitised parts removed.

photograph An image produced by the action of light on a chemically prepared surface.

photogravure A method of photoengraving in which the design etched on the metal surface is sunk into the surface, not relief.

photolithography The lithographic printing method in which plates are prepared photographically rather than by hand. See also **offset lithography.**

photomechanical transfer A method of quickly producing a photographic print or plate by a chemical transfer process; the print or plate produced by this method. Also *PMT.*

photopolymer A light-sensitive polymer (plastic) that is used for making printing plates, the non-image areas of the plate being chemically dissolved to leave a relief image area.

photoprint A photographic reproduction of an image.

photosensitive Sensitive to electromagnetic radiation, especially light.

photosetting See **phototypesetting.**

Photostat® A kind of machine for making positive or negative photographic copies.

phototypesetting The production of type images on photosensitive paper or film by optical means instead of casting characters by a hot-metal process. The composition is usually undertaken by means of a keyboard linked to a computer to set the text to the required typeface, size, measure, and with the appropriate hyphenation and justification.

pi character (*US*) See **special sort.**

pica (1) The standard unit of measurement of typeset material, 4.23mm (about one-sixth of an inch) or 12 points. Also known as **em; pica em.** (2) A measurement of typewriter typesize, ten characters to the horizontal inch.

picking The lifting of surface fibres of paper during printing, caused by sticky ink or poor-quality paper.

pictogram A stylised picture used as a symbol or sign. Also known as **pictograph.**

picture library A resource that contains a collection of photographs which may be used, for a payment and with due acknowledgment, for reproduction in a book, magazine, etc.

picture research The finding of suitable illustrative material for reproduction in a book, magazine, etc.

pie Jumbled typeset type.

pigment Substance used for colouring.

pirate To publish a book without permission, infringing the owner's copyright.

pitch The number of characters that will fit into one inch of a line of text, typically 10, 12, or 15 when the typed text is monospaced.

pixel One of the minute units that make up the picture of an electronically produced colour image.

plagiarism The act of taking the thoughts or writings of another person and using them as one's own.

planning The imposing of film onto a grid.

planographic Of a method of printing from a flat surface, e.g. lithography, rather than from a surface that is raised or sunken.

plastic-comb binding See **mechanical binding.**

plate (1) A printing surface, of metal, plastic, rubber, etc., from which an impression is taken in printing. The cylinder that bears the plate on a printing press is known as the plate cylinder. (2) An illustration separately printed, usually on different paper, and insetted in a book.

platen press A small letterpress printing machine in which the paper is pushed against the type.

PMT Abbreviation of **photomechanical transfer.**

point A measurement of typesize: in the UK and USA, 1 point equalling 0.01383 in (0.3515 mm), 12 points making 0.166 in (one-sixth of an inch, i.e. one pica or pica em), and 72 one inch. In the rest of Europe, the point (or Didot point) is 0.0148 in (0.376 mm), and 12 points, 0.1776 in, making a unit called the cicero. See also **body size.**

portrait A book or illustration with a height greater than its width. Contrast with *landscape.*

positive A photographic film, in which the lights and shades and colours are unchanged from the original.

poster A large notice or advertisement stuck in a public place.

preface An introduction to a book usually written by the author.

preliminary pages See **prelims.**

prelims The preliminary pages of a book, comprising the half-title, title, dedication, contents, etc., before the main part of the book. Also known as **front matter.**

presentation visual See **visual.**

press (1) A printing press. (2) A printing or publishing organisation. (3) Newspapers, magazines, etc., considered collectively.

press agent A person who arranges for newspaper advertising and publicity.

press-cutting agency An organisation that provides publishers with articles, especially reviews, about the publisher's books from general, trade, etc., newspapers and periodicals.

press proofs   The final proof that is taken before text, illustrations, etc., are printed, and which provides the standard against which the print-machine operator tests the output of the press.

press release   A statement giving information about something, sent or given to newspapers, reporters, etc.

primary colours   See **process colours.**

print-out   The reproduction of text (printed paper output) on paper which a computer produces via a printer.

print run   The number of copies printed at a single printing.

print to paper   An instruction that the quantity of paper available should be printed, rather than setting a precise number of copies to be printed.

printable   (Of the quality of paper) fit for printing on.

printer   (1) An output device from a computer which produces hard copy (text on paper).   (2) (In colour separation) the device that produces a single colour.

printer's error   An error that is the fault of the typesetter, not the author or publisher. Also *PE*.

printing head   The part of the printer (the output device on a computer) that actually does the printing of characters, numbers, and symbols onto the paper. Types of printing head can be golfball, daisy wheel, or dot-matrix.

printing history   The details of the date of original publication and the dates of any subsequent reprints or further editions.

printing press   Any of various machines by which impressions are taken in ink on paper from types, plates, etc. For the different printing processes see **gravure; letterpress; offset lithography;** etc.

pro forma invoice   An invoice that has to be paid before goods will be delivered.

process camera   A specially designed camera for use in graphic design work, used in half-tones, line artwork, and, with filters, colour separations.

process colours   The standard colours cyan (blue), magenta (red), and yellow, that, with black, are fundamental to four-colour printing. Almost all colours can be obtained by using inks of the process colours in the correct proportions.

process engraving   A photomechanical method of making relief blocks or plates for the printing of illustrations.

production department   The activities of a publisher concerned with the manufacturing of books for publication, including the calculation of the extent of a book, the passing of the edited marked-up manuscript to a typesetter, the coordination of proofs, the ordering of paper, etc., and the printing, binding, and delivery of books.

program   The set of instructions that a computer carries out in sequence, enabling the computer to operate and carry out specific tasks.

progressive proofs; progressives   Colour proofs that show each colour printed on its own and also combined with the preceding colour in stages.

promotion   Special effort, such as a free sample or a money-off offer, aimed at increasing purchases by consumers.

proof   One or more early impressions printed for the purpose of correcting errors. Also known as **pull.**

proofreading   The checking of proofs and the marking of corrections on proofs. For the standard proof correction marks, see Appendix.

proportional spacing   The spacing of typewritten characters in proportion to their size. Standard typewriters produce letters of uniform width, e.g. a capital L gets the same space as a lower case l, irrespective of their size.

Typewriters which offer a facility for proportional spacing allow less space for a small l than the space they allow for a capital L.

proud   Projecting slightly from the surrounding area.

pseudonym   A false name used by an author.

public lending right   The right of authors to receive payment when their books are borrowed from public libraries.

public relations   (1) The department of a company or institution that works to improve relationships with the public.   (2) The goodwill, favourable relationships, etc., between a company or institution and the public.

publication date   The publisher's official date that a book becomes available for sale.

published price   The price a publisher sets for a book. See also **net book; non-net book.**

publisher   The company, individual, etc., that is responsible for the issuing and offering for sale of books. For the individual aspects of the activities of a publisher, see entries at **design; editorial work; marketing department; production department; sales department;** etc.

pull   One or more early impressions printed for the purpose of correcting errors. Also known as **proof.**

pull-out   See **fold-out.**

pulp   The soft mass obtained from the breaking and grinding of rags, wood, etc., before it is made chemically or mechanically into paper.

pulp board   Board, usually single ply, made from pulp.

Qq

quad (1) (In hot-metal composition) a piece of type-metal lower than the letters, used in spacing between words and filling out blank lines. (2) (In phototypesetting) the action of spacing out a line. (3) A size of paper four times the normal size. The size is taken by doubling each dimension of the standard sheet, e.g. medium 18 in × 23 in, quad medium 36 in × 46 in.

quarter binding; quarter bound A hardback binding in which the back (spine) is covered with a stronger material than the different material, often paper, used to cover the sides.

quarto (1) Having the sheet folded into four leaves or eight pages, usually written 4to. (2) A book, or the size of a book, made up of such sheets. (3) See **paper sizes.**

quire 24 or 25 sheets of paper.

quoins The wedges or expandable devices used for locking type, blocks, etc., in a chase (metal frame).

quotation (1) A commercial document sent to the purchaser from the supplier quoting the costs of items, discounts available, transport details, any additional charges to be levied, terms of business and for how long the prices/terms will hold. (2) A passage or phrase from a book, play, etc., that is repeated exactly by someone else.

quotation marks The single (' ') or double (" ") inverted commas used to show the beginning and end of a quotation. When single marks are used, double marks are used to show a quotation within a quotation and vice versa. Also known as **inverted commas; quotes.**

qv   Abbreviation of *quod vide*, a Latin expression meaning 'which see', used to show a cross-reference.

qwerty keyboard   A keyboard which has the keys laid out as that used on standard typewriters. The word derives from the letters at the top left-hand side of the keyboard.

Rr

ragged left/right Typesetting of material in which the lines are not aligned (are unjustified) at the left/right ends of the line.

RAM Abbreviation of *random access memory*, memory into which information can be written and from which it may be read in a random access fashion. The size of a computer's random access memory is a measure of the computer's power.

range To align, e.g. characters, or lines of type. Ranged left/right means that the text is aligned at the left/right margin.

ranging numerals Arabic numbers that are of equal height, aligning at the top and bottom: 0123, etc. Contrast with *non-ranging figures*. Also known as **lining figures.**

rare books Books that are less than 75 years old and are unavailable from the publisher.

re-issue To republish a book that was previously out of print.

read only memory See **ROM.**

reader (1) A person, especially someone working at a printer's, who corrects proofs. (2) A person who reads and reports on manuscripts for a publisher.

ream A quantity of paper, now usually 500 sheets; also 480 or 516 sheets.

rebind (1) The binding of a stored second or later set of printed sheets of a book. (2) To replace a defective binding with a good one.

recto   The right-hand page of an open book. Contrast with *verso*.

reduction   The process of making a photograph, illustration, etc., smaller in reproduction; the amount by which the photograph, etc., is made smaller.

reel-fed   See **web-fed.**

reference marks   Signs used in a text that refer to footnotes, used especially in the order * † ‡ § ¶ ‖, repeated in duplicate (**, etc.) if necessary.

references   A list of books, periodicals, etc., referred to. References may be listed at the bottom of the page, at the end of each chapter, or at the end of the book.

register   The state of being correctly aligned or in its proper position (*in register*) or incorrectly aligned or not in its proper position (*out of register*), as in colour printing or when pages back one another. Register marks (crosses, triangles, etc.) are used to show correct alignment when different elements are superimposed.

relief printing   A printing process such as letterpress that uses a raised ink surface to produce the printed image.

remainder   A book, the sales of which have fallen off, that is sold at a reduced price by the publisher to the bookseller who then offers the book to the public at less than the original published price.

representative   See **sales representative.**

reprint   To print a new impression of a book, especially with little or no change.

repro   (1) Abbreviation of **repro pull.**   (2) Abbreviation of **reproduction.**

repro pull   A reproduction proof, of a quality good enough to be suitable for reproduction photographically. Also known as **reproduction proof; reproduction pull.**

reproduction   The copying of an image.

reprography   The process of obtaining copies from a master copy, e.g. spirit duplicating, ink stencil duplicating, and all forms of photocopying and carbon copying.

rescreen   To screen a half-tone, rather than reproducing it dot for dot.

resolution   The definition of a visual image in producing clear fine details.

retainer   A fee paid to someone to make certain that he or she is available for work when needed.

retouching   Work done by hand, especially on a photograph by pencil-work on the negative, to enhance the image or remove imperfections.

returns   Unsold books, newspapers, etc., returned by a bookseller to a publisher.

reversal film   A photographic film that gives a positive image after being processed.

reverse indent   See **hanging indentation.**

reverse left to right   To reproduce an image so that it appears as it would in a mirror.

reverse out   To reproduce text, lines, etc., as white on a background of black (or another colour) rather than black on white.

reverse reading   Text that reads backwards, as from right to left, e.g. in settings in letterpress printing.

review copy   A copy of a book sent to a newspaper, magazine, etc., for review.

review slip   A small enclosure sent with a review copy of a book, with information including the book's title, author, publication date, and price. The review slip often also contains a request for a copy of the publication in which the review appears to be sent to the publisher.

revise   A further proof in which corrections have been incorporated.

RI   Abbreviation of *re-issue*, response of a publisher to a bookseller that a book ordered is being re-issued, with the date of re-issue as shown.

right-angle fold   The folding of sheets with two or more folds, each fold being at right angles to the previous one.

right reading   Text that reads normally, as from left to right, e.g. in settings in offset lithography.

rights   The legal entitlement to publish and sell a book. *Volume rights* describe the publisher's right during the full term of copyright to produce and publish the work in all editions in the stated parts of the world, and also to publish other editions, e.g. paperback, and to control the publishing rights that may be leased to another publisher. *Subsidiary rights* include translation rights, book-club rights, serial rights, broadcast rights, and merchandising rights. If a publisher allows the book to go out of print, all rights that have not been leased by the publisher revert to the author.

ring binder   A loose-leaf binder which has metal rings that can be opened to hold perforated sheets of paper.

river   An apparent wide flow of white that runs down a page of printed matter, caused by the poor spacing of words.

ROM   Abbreviation of *read only memory*, a store of memory from which information can only be read or copied. Read only memory is usually a permanent store holding software which is permanently or firmly in place.

rom   Abbreviation of **roman.**

roman   (Of type) of the ordinary upright kind, not italic.

Roman numerals   The system of letters used by the Romans to represent numbers: I (one), V (five), X (ten), L (fifty), C (hundred), D (five hundred), M (thousand).

Lower-case Roman numerals are often used to show the page numbers of the preliminary pages of a book.

rotary press   A printing press in which a curved printing plate is attached to a cylinder that rotates against the paper.

rotogravure   A photogravure printing process using a rotary process.

rough   A rough sketch to give an impression of the original, or a drawing which needs to be redrawn.

round and back   The bookbinding process that gives a convex shaped back and a concave appearance to the edge of a book opposite the spine.

round brackets   See **parentheses.**

royal   See **book sizes; paper sizes.**

royalty   The payment to an author for every copy of a book sold, often expressed as a percentage of the publisher's selling price or net receipts.

RP   Abbreviation of *reprinting,* a response by a publisher to a bookseller for a copy of a book that is not at that time available. *RP* may be followed by an abbreviation of the month or number indicating the month, e.g. RP/Mar or RP/3, to show that the reprinted copies are expected to be available in, e.g. March.

ruby   A former size of printing type, approximately equal to 5½ points. US equivalent: *agate.*

rule   A continuous printed line.

run   (1) To print.   (2) To carry out a computer program or routine.

run-around   The setting of printed text in such a way that the column width is made narrower in order to allow for an illustration to be fitted in.

run on   (1) To continue the printed text without a break, with no new paragraph. US equivalent: *run in.*   (2) To continue to operate a printing machine after completing an initial order for sheets.

running head   A heading, as one which changes from page to page, e.g. in dictionaries to give the first and last entries. Running heads may stay the same throughout the book, giving the title of the book on a left-hand page and the chapter heading on a right-hand page. When such headings appear at the foot of a page they are called *running feet*.

running text   The body of main text that continues from one page to the next, in contrast to the fixed positions for illustrations, footnotes, etc.

Ss

saddle-stitch To stitch, normally with wire, through the back fold of insetted work, a method of binding used for brochures.

sale or return An arrangement by which a bookseller pays only for the books sold, those that are not sold being returned to the supplier.

sales department The department responsible for selling a firm's products. The sales department can include: advertising, marketing, and after-sales service.

sales representative The person who represents the publisher in a sales capacity and negotiates, with possible customers, especially bookshops, sales offers in the name of the company. He or she has a geographical territory to cover.

sans serif A style of typeface without serifs.

SBN See **ISBN.**

sc Abbreviation of *small capitals*: A B C, etc., that align with the x-height; indicated by double underlining on a manuscript.

scale To determine the necessary reduction or enlargement of an illustration to enable it to fit into a given area.

scanner An electronic device used mostly in colour separation, in which a high-intensity light or laser beam scans an original transparency or artwork. Signals are sent in digital form via colour filters to a computer that prepares screened negatives or positive film for each of the four colours.

scatter proof   A proof of several illustrations in any position, without regard to the correct position in the layout.

schedule   A list of all the different stages in the production of a book, with a note of the date by which each stage should be completed.

score   To impress a mark on board or thicker paper to make the folding easier.

screen   A sheet of glass or film that has a grid, used in the half-tone photographic process to divide an image into dots. The fineness of the screen is represented in lines per inch or lines per centimetre. For example a 133 screen (per inch) is 54 screen (per centimetre). To *screen* is to photograph an image through a screen.

screen angle   The angle at which a screen needs to be set to avoid the moiré effect when superimposing different screen patterns. The angles often used are: black 45°, magenta 75°, yellow 90°, and cyan 105°.

screen printing   A printing process that uses a fine mesh of cloth with a stencil treated so that the areas not to be printed are impervious. Ink is then forced through the screen onto the paper behind.

script   A typeface that resembles handwriting.

scrolling   The movement of text up and down or across a visual display unit so that the user can view the whole of a document or, on systems that display only half pages, the whole of a page.

search   An examination of information in a computer file to find the occurrence of a character, word, or phrase. A search of a document is normally carried out from the place where the cursor is positioned to the end of a document.

search and replace   A word processing facility in which every occurrence of a specified character, word, or phrase is replaced with a pre-defined character, word, or phrase.

section (1) A folded section of pages made from one sheet. Also known as **signature.** (2) A division of a book, especially the subdivision of a chapter.

section mark The mark § used as a reference mark, especially to a footnote.

see safe An agreement that states that a supplier will give credit for unsold books returned by the end of a specified period. In some arrangements all the goods must be paid for when originally supplied.

see-through The degree to which the printed image of one side of the paper is visible on the other side of the paper. Also known as **show-through.**

self-cover A booklet whose cover is made of the same material as the paper used in the rest of the booklet.

self-ends Endpapers that are formed from the first and last sections of the book.

separate A printing of a single article from a periodical. Also known as **offprint.**

separated artwork Artwork that is made up of a series of overlays, each overlay standing for a single colour.

separation See **colour separation.**

serial rights Rights to publish one or more extracts of a book in a periodical or magazine, especially before a book is published (first serial rights).

series A set of books in the same format and dealing with related subjects, issued by the same publisher.

serif The finishing stroke at the top and bottom of a letter.

set (1) To arrange type by hand into words and lines. (2) The width of an individual character of type. Also known as **set width.** (3) A number of books that are grouped together to form a unit.

set-off The unwanted transfer of ink from one newly printed sheet to another.

set solid   Describing type set without the insertion of space (leading) between the lines.

sewing   The sewing of pages in each section and then to join the sections to one another.

shadow   The darkest part of a photographic half-tone reproduction.

shank   The rectangular piece of metal that carries a character from which an inked print can be made. See **body** (1).

sheet   A sheet which has not been folded.

sheet-fed   Of a printing press that prints single sheets of paper separately, in contrast to *web-fed*.

sheet stock   Printed sheets that have not yet been bound.

sheet work   The printing of the two sides of a sheet with different formes.

shelf talker   A prominent card advertising a book in a shop, positioned on the shelf where the book is displayed.

short page   A page that is one or two lines shorter to avoid an unsightly break.

shoulder   (1) The slight protuberance down either side of the spine of a book caused by rounding and backing, and against which the front and back covers fit tightly. (2) The flat surface on a piece of type, from which the face rises.

shout   A bold prominently displayed statement describing a book, printed for example on the book's cover.

show-through   The degree to which the printed image of one side of the paper is visible on the other side. Also known as **see-through.**

showcard   A point-of-sale display, advertising goods. It is generally placed on a table or sales counter.

shrink-wrap   To wrap a book in a transparent plastic film that is then shrunk when heated to produce a closely sealed pack suitable for display.

side-stitch   To sew through the side of a book from front to back near the spine with a thread, wire, or staples. Also known as **side-sew; stab-stitch.**

signature   (1) A letter or figure at the foot of the first page (and usually on one or more successive pages) of each sheet in a book, indicating the order in which the sheets should be bound.   (2) A folded section of pages comprising one sheet so marked.

signing session   The organised visit of an author to a bookshop when his or her book is published in order to sign purchased copies of the book.

silhouette   An outline drawing of a person, especially when seen from the side and filled in with black.

silk-screen printing   A printing process that uses a fine mesh of cloth, originally silk, with a stencil treated so that the areas not to be printed are impervious. Ink is then forced through the screen onto the paper behind.

single drum duplicator   A duplicating machine consisting of a drum made of perforated metal covered with fabric, containing ink squeezed into it from a tube through the filler hole. As the drum rotates, ink is spread evenly through the fabric, transferring the image from the stencil onto paper. Compare with *twin drum duplicator.*

sixteenmo   (1) Having 16 leaves to the sheet, usually written 16mo.   (2) A book, or the size of a book, made up of such sheets.

size   A gluey mixture that is used to seal the surface of paper.

slash   The stroke /. See **solidus.**

slip case   A protective case to hold one or more books so that only the spines are visible.

slip proof   See **galley.**

sloped roman   See **italic.**

slug   A solid line of metal type cast by a composing machine.

small capitals   The capital letters A, B, C, etc., that align with the x-height; indicated by double underlining on a manuscript, galley proof, etc.

small offset   An offset lithography printing machine that prints paper below about A2 in size.

small order   An order that is of insufficient value to justify the handling costs. Sometimes a publisher imposes a surcharge for such an order.

smashing   The compressing of folded signatures in binding to make them more compact for binding, by expelling air.

soft copy   Computer output on a medium which cannot be read by an observer, e.g. floppy disk or computer output as displayed on the screen of a visual display unit.

soft-cover   Bound in flexible covers, especially paperback.

soft hyphen   In word processing and computer typesetting, a hyphen inserted into a word that is broken at the end of a line. A soft hyphen is automatically removed if the word changes its position to appear on one line only.

solid   Describing type set without the insertion of spaces (leading) between the lines.

solidus   The stroke / used to separate alternatives, ratios, and to show breaks in lines of verse. Also known as **oblique; slash; stroke; virgule.**

sort   (1) One character of type.   (2) To arrange items into meaningful order, often alphabetical, numerical, or chronological.

space   The interval between lines or words.

special sort   An unusual character, or a character which is not part of the standard fount. US equivalent: *pi character*.

specification   (1) The detailed description of the size, style, etc., of the typefaces that the designer determines for each book. Also known as **type spec.**   (2) The detailed instruction for any of various other tasks, such as reproducing illustrations or printing and finishing.

specimen   A specimen page or specimen pages giving examples of all the general typographical styles, sizes, headings, etc., that a printer will encounter in setting a particular book.

spelling check   A computer program that uses a standard or specialised dictionary which can be added to by the user. When the program is run, the text is checked for spelling errors offering the user the opportunity to make corrections.

spine   The back bound edge of a book, usually printed with the book's title, author, and publisher.

spine out   (Of books) displayed on a shelf with the spine facing outwards.

spinner   A revolving stand for displaying books for sale.

spiral binding   See **mechanical binding.**

spirit duplicator   A machine used to produce multiple copy documents by the preparation of a master. The master is prepared by typing or writing on master paper against which a sheet of hectographic carbon is placed enabling a reversed image to be obtained on the back of the master paper. The master is then fixed to the drum of the duplicator and as the drum is rotated, sheets of non-absorbent duplicating paper are fed through, damped with a fluid which activates a dye on the master, transferring the image the correct way round onto the duplicating paper.

split screen The displaying of more than one image on the screen of a VDU, e.g. a page of text may be shown in one section of the screen, whilst a page of a spreadsheet may be shown in a different area of the same screen at the same time. Areas of the screen are referred to as *windows*.

spoilage The inevitable wastage of materials in the printing process. US equivalent: *makeover*.

spotting The painting out of imperfections on photographs, artwork, negative film, etc.

spread A table, illustration, etc., which extends across an opening.

spreadsheet A computer program that allows the visual display unit of the computer to act as rows and columns of analysis paper. This allows the user to enter sets of figures that can be altered and manipulated. This type of program is typically used for accounting, budgeting, and evaluating different financial policies.

square back A form of sewn binding with a square spine, where the book has not been rounded and backed.

square brackets The pair of characters [ ] used to enclose an editorial comment or explanation in quoted matter and as brackets within parentheses (round brackets). Square brackets are known by typesetters and printers simply as *brackets*.

s/s Abbreviation of *same size*: an instruction that an illustration should be reproduced at the same size as the original.

stab-stitch See **side-stitch.**

stamping (*US*) (In bookbinding) the impressing of letters or designs on a book cover using ink or metal foil.

standing type Type or plates that are stored after printing and are kept ready for further printing.

stem The main upright stroke of a letter.

stencil (1) A *thermal* stencil is produced on a thermal photocopier. It enables diagrams and pictures to be reproduced in ink because it is a photocopied procedure. (2) An *electronic* stencil is produced by placing a vinyl stencil on a scanner which burns tiny holes into it to produce an exact replica of the original document, photograph, or diagram as a series of tiny holes through which ink will penetrate. (3) Manufacturers have produced a *lightweight* stencil to be produced on a letter-quality printer (using a daisy wheel print element) attached to a word processing station.

stencil duplicator See **ink duplicator.**

step and repeat The multiple exposure of an image in a preset horizontally or vertically stepping sequence.

step index An index in which alphabetical guides are set down the outer edge of the pages.

stereotype A duplicate printing plate that is cast from a plastic, rubber, papier mâché, etc., mould of movable type or other relief printing material; the method of making such plates. Also known as **stereo.**

stet A Latin word meaning 'let it stand', used to restore text after marking for deletion, an instruction indicated to the printer by a row of dots below the text which is to be restored.

stitch To sew all the sections of a book together. See **saddle-stitch; side-stitch.**

STM Abbreviation of *scientific, technical, and medical,* a category of academic books.

stock (1) Paper that is used in printing. (2) Copies of books that are not yet sold.

stock control Making sure that there is always enough stock available for the production processes, etc., recording and analysis of sales, and arranging for the efficient and regular replacement of stock as it is used up.

stocktaking   The counting of stock in order to arrive at an estimate of the total value of stocks held. Stocktaking can be done annually, six monthly, etc., depending upon the requirements of the organisation.

stone   The level, usually metal, surface on which pages are made up into printing formes.

strawboard   Thick stiff cardboard made of straw pulp or waste, used mainly for making book covers.

streamer   A headline in large type that extends across the full width of a newspaper page.

strike-on   Composition on a typewriter using a carbon ribbon, or with another keyboard machine—often a more sophisticated machine with proportional spacing and automatic justification—that makes a physical impression on the paper.

strike-through   The penetration of ink through paper.

strip in   To join the ends of two pieces of film or paper, as in phototypesetting, the correction of minor typesetting errors by cutting out and replacing of the film.

stripping   The process of assembling film into a page.

stroke   The character /. See **solidus.**

sub-edit   To edit material, especially for newspapers, in preparation for printing. See also **copy-editing.**

subhead   The heading to part of a chapter. Also known as **subheading.**

subscribe   (Of booksellers) to order copies of a book before it is published, the level of such orders being known as *subscription.*

subscript   A character which lies below the normal line of type (the base line), e.g. the number 2 in H_2O, CO_2.

subsidiary rights   See **rights.**

substance   (1) (In UK) the weight expressed in grams of a sheet of paper with an area of one square metre. See

gm². (2) (In USA) the weight in pounds of a ream of paper of a certain standard size, usually 25 in × 38 in.

subtractive primaries The colours cyan (a blue), magenta (a red), and yellow. When combined, these colours make black.

subtractive process A photographic process in which all but the colours that are wanted are taken out by passing the light through special filters.

summary A shortened version of a text, giving only the main points.

supercalender To give a very smooth finish to paper. See also **calender.**

superior Of a small letter or number set above the x-height, e.g. the number 2 in 3². Such a letter or number is also known as a **superscript.**

supplement An additional part of a publication to give corrections or new information.

swash (Of letters) italic, with decorative strokes that end in an elaborate flourish.

swatch A collection of samples showing different colours.

swung dash The sign ~ used to represent a word that has already been printed.

symbol A sign used to represent something, e.g. + meaning 'plus', and ☎ meaning 'telephone number'.

synopsis A short summary or outline of a book.

Tt

tab index   An index in which alphabetical guides are attached to the outer edge of the pages.

tabloid   A page that is half the size of a broadsheet. The term is commonly used to refer to a newspaper with a format approximately 12 in × 16 in (300 mm × 400 mm) that contains a great deal of photographic material.

tabular   Of the setting of material, especially numbers, in rows and columns.

tabulate   To set or arrange in tabular form.

tack   The stickiness of ink, a varnish, or adhesive.

tail   The bottom edge of a page.

tail margin   The space that is between the printed area and the bottom of the page.

tailpiece   A decorative design at the bottom of a page or the end of a chapter.

take   The amount of material given to a typesetter.

take back   An instruction to a typesetter to move text to the previous line or to the previous page.

take in   An instruction to a typesetter to include additional text that is provided.

take over   An instruction to a typesetter to begin the text on the next line rather than run it on to the present line.

tape   (1) (In binding) a strip of strong material laid across the spine to help reinforce the joint of a case-bound book.   (2) (In some mechanical composition systems) a strip of paper in which typesetting data is represented by small holes punched in rows across the tape.

Teleordering   A system by which bookshops order books via one central computer that then passes on the orders to the supplier. Bookshops enter orders into a computer keyboard during the day. Overnight all the terminals are called by the central computer to extract the day's orders. After checking the information, orders are then consolidated and forwarded to the appropriate publisher, distributor, or wholesaler.

teleprinter   Resembling a typewriter, a device which is connected to a telephone line enabling messages at one end to be simultaneously reproduced on a machine at another end.

teletex   A development of teleprinters, teletex is a system which transmits data between terminals at high speed over the telephone network, combining text editing with high speed telex-related equipment.

teletext   Broadcast videotext. Information is carried from a computer to a receiver by radio waves where pages of information are displayed on a screen, the screen capable of being changed by a push-button selection device. The two systems of this type in operation in the UK are Ceefax (British Broadcasting Corporation) and Oracle (Independent Broadcasting Authority).

telex   A fully automatic teleprinter allowing interconnection between terminals over a dedicated network permitting communication in print. Each installation has an individual number and can identify itself by means of an answer back code.

Temp   Abbreviation of *temporary* or *temporarily*, as in *Temp OS*, a reply by a publisher to a bookseller that a book is temporarily out of stock.

template   A thin flat piece of metal, plastic, etc., cut in a certain shape, used as a pattern by drawing or marking round it.

terminal   A peripheral device consisting of a keyboard and screen, linked to a computer used to input data and receive output from the computer, or for sending and receiving data over a communications channel.

terms The conditions of an agreement between a publisher and a bookshop, etc.,—concerning for example the discounts given—or between a publisher and an author.

text The main written or printed words in a book, in contrast to the preliminary matter, headings, illustrations, etc.

text area The area on a page occupied by the text and the notes (it may or may not include the headline and page number).

text editing The editing of text on a computer, often within word processing. It may be carried out on any form of computer from a mainframe with appropriate software to a dedicated word processor.

text processing Computer editing and subsequent production of text. Often used as a synonym for word processing, although text processing more commonly refers to the handling of very large quantities of text.

textbook A book used in teaching, giving the main facts of a subject.

TF Abbreviation of *to follow shortly*, used as a reply by a publisher to a bookshop, for example in *OO/TF*, meaning 'on order, to follow shortly'.

thermal heat copier A process using heat instead of light to form a copy of an image with the use of a special heat sensitive copy paper. Although it is a very rapid method of copying, a disadvantage is that a thermal copier will not copy images unless they have a carbon or metallic content in them. Also known as **thermographic copier**.

thermal printer A method of printing using paper coated with a dye that darkens at predetermined temperatures to produce a copy of an image.

thermographic copier A method of photocopying where heat is applied to the paper bearing the copy image to fuse the ink to the paper. As the ink is fused, it swells and the copy is produced with an embossed appearance. Also known as **thermal heat copier.**

thermography Any process of writing or printing involving the use of heat, for example coating a printed image with a powder that becomes fused with the ink when heated to give a glossy raised image.

thermoplastic binding The binding of collated sections of a book with a hot plastic glue that hardens when cooled.

thick space A space of one-third of a set em.

thin space A space of one-fifth of a set em.

thirtytwomo (1) Having 32 leaves to the sheet, usually written 32mo. (2) A book, or the size of a book, made up of such sheets.

thread sewing The sewing of collated sections of a book individually then to each other before the case is applied.

throw-out See **fold-out.**

thumb index An index that gives the letters of the alphabet arranged as indentations on the outer margins of the pages of a book.

tilde The sign ˜ used over an *n* in Spanish to indicate the sound *ny*.

tint A pattern of dots or lines or a solid panel in a second colour, which can be laid down on artwork and reproduced as line artwork.

tip in To paste a plate, errata slip, etc., to the adjoining page, rather than binding it in with the other pages.

title (1) An individual published literary work, as in a publisher's catalogue. (2) The name of a book, play, etc., or a heading, for example of a chapter, in such a work.

title-page A right-hand page at the front of a book giving the book's title, author, and publisher.

titling A fount of capital letters, with no lower-case letters, used in headings.

to view Stating the number of pages that are printed on one side of a sheet.

tone The shades of dark and light in an image relative to each other.

toner The substance used to develop an image in electrostatic copying. See also **xerographic copier.**

tooling The impressing of a design on the cover of a book by hand, using for example heated tools.

TOP Abbreviation of *temporarily out of print*, a reply by a publisher to a bookseller to an order for a book.

TOS Abbreviation of *temporarily out of stock*, a reply by a publisher to a bookseller to an order for a book.

trade counter The department in a warehouse, etc., where a publisher's books, especially in small orders, are supplied to bookshops.

trade discount A discount, usually a percentage of the published price, allowed by a publisher to a wholesaler or retail bookshop.

trade edition An edition of a book intended to be sold through the usual trade outlets to the general public, in contrast to, for example, an edition for schools or a book club.

trade journal A periodical with articles of interest and information on a particular specialist trade.

transfer diffusion copier An office copier which creates a negative when light shines through an original to the exposed areas of a negative sheet. The negative and positive sheets are both passed face to face through a bath of developer fluid which causes a replica of the original to be transferred from the negative to the positive paper. This machine can also produce translucent masters for use on a dyeline copier.

transfer lettering Lettering on the back of a plastic sheet that can be rubbed down onto paper, etc., when preparing artwork.

transparency (1) A photograph, especially a positive colour image, printed on transparent material and seen by shining light through it or projecting it onto a screen. (2) A sheet of acetate paper onto which diagrams may be drawn or documents photocopied for use in conjunction with an overhead projector.

transpose To change the order of characters, words, paragraphs, etc.

trim To cut a sheet of paper to the desired size after printing, and in removing the folds to separate pages at the top, bottom, and outer edge.

trim marks The marks on a printed sheet to show where the paper is to be trimmed. US equivalent: *cut marks*.

trimmed page size; trim size The final page size of paper, as in a book.

trs Abbreviation of *transpose*, to change the order of characters, words, paragraphs, etc.

true italic See **italic.**

turned Printed upside down or on its side, either correctly or wrongly. A *turned comma* is a single inverted comma '.

turnovers All the lines in a paragraph except the first.

twentyfourmo (1) Having 24 leaves to the sheet, usually written 24mo. (2) A book, or the size of a book, made up of such sheets.

twice up Material that is prepared at two times the size that it will finally appear.

twin drum duplicator   A duplicator consisting of two drums which are connected by fabric. The fabric is inked by a roller with the ink being pumped from a tube attached to the machine. Compare with *single drum duplicator.*

two/three up   Printing in which two/three multiples of the same image are printed on a larger sheet in a single operation, in order to use a press to a greater capacity.

type   (In letterpress printing) the rectangular piece of metal on one end of which is cast or engraved a character.

type area   The area on a page occupied by the text and the notes (it may or may not include the headline and page number). Also known as **type page.**

type-height   The standard overall height of letterpress type, 0.918 in (23.3 mm). Also known as **type-high.**

type page   See **type area.**

type scale   A ruler marked with ems, points, etc., used for measuring type widths, the depth of a page, etc. US equivalent: *line gauge.*

type spec   The detailed description of the size, style, etc., of the typefaces that the designer determines for each book. Also known as **specification.**

typeface   The printing surface of a type cut into one of a variety of styles.

typescript   Typewritten material.

typesetting   The setting of type especially by photo-typesetting, in which type images are optically produced on a sensitive paper or film, or by hot-metal typesetting, in which type is cast from molten metal.

typewriter   A machine used to prepare printed documents with letters and numbers usually in the same style and with a consistent size, shape, and alignment. On some typewriters, characters are spaced according to the size of the characters (see **proportional spacing**). On golfball typewriters the print element can be changed to give a different typeface design.

typo   A wrong letter in printed or typed matter resulting from a mistake by a typesetter.

typographer   (*US*) A person who sets type.

typography   The art, style, design, etc., of using type effectively to give a pleasing legible appearance.

Uu

u and lc; u/lc   Abbreviation of *upper and lower case*, i.e. to be set as capitals and small letters.

uc   Abbreviation of *upper case*.

umlaut   In German, the two dots placed over a letter representing a vowel change, e.g. ü, ö.

unbacked   Printed on only one side of the paper.

underexpose   To expose a film, plate, etc., to too little light.

underlay   To bring a block, forme, etc., to type-height by putting material such as card under it.

underline   (1) A caption to an illustration.   (2) The placing of a line under typeset matter: a wavy underline indicates bold, one straight line indicates italic, two straight lines indicate small capitals, and three straight lines indicate capitals.

unit   The body width of a letter, usually one em = 18 units or one en = 9 units, the size of the unit varying according to the different sizes of type.

unit cost   The cost of producing one copy of a book, used as a basis for working out the book's selling price, and calculated by dividing the total costs of producing the book by the number of copies produced.

unjustified   Text which is aligned at one margin only, usually the left-hand margin, and ragged (uneven), at the other. The lines of type are therefore of unequal length.

unsewn binding   See **perfect binding.**

UPC   Abbreviation of *Universal Product Code*; see **bar code**.

upper case   A capital letter: A, in contrast to lower case: a, and small capitals: A. Upper case letters are shown on a manuscript, galley proof, etc., by three lines under the relevant character. See also **case** (2).

Vv

Vandyke   See **Ozalid.**

vanity publishing   The publishing of books by a company (a *vanity publisher*) at the author's expense.

variable space   A space that can vary in extent between words, used especially in justifying text.

variant; variant reading   One or more words and/or punctuation marks in an early version of a text which differ from the final version.

Varityper®   A kind of machine with interchangeable typeface founts which allow one to prepare material as on a typewriter and also to place the lettering in an appropriate style, size, and shape to make an impressive presentation.

varnish   A transparent protective coating to produce a glossy finish.

VDU   Abbreviation of *visual display unit*, a cathode-ray tube on which the output of a computer can be displayed.

vehicle   A substance, e.g. linseed oil, in which the pigment of printing ink is mixed.

vellum   A finer kind of parchment from the skin of calves, kids, or lambs.

venture   A business activity whose outcome is uncertain. It is often the case that more than one person or company is involved, so that the risks (and profits) are shared.

verso   The left-hand page of an open book. Contrast with *recto.*

vertical integration   A situation in which a company merges with (or takes over) another company which is involved in a different stage of producing the same thing. A hardback publisher buying a paperback publisher is an example of vertical integration.

vide   A Latin word meaning 'see', used to direct a reader to a certain place, e.g. *vide infra* (see below), *vide supra* (see above).

video disk   A disk containing recorded visual and sound information which can be played on a video recorder and transmitted to a television screen. In contrast to tapes in video cassettes, some video disks offer random access.

viewdata   An electronic system facilitating computer based information to be available via a VDU or appropriately adapted television set. There are two categories of viewdata systems: *Broadcast videotex* where information is carried from the computer to the receiver by radio waves enabling a limited number of pages to be displayed on a screen using a push-button selection device, e.g. Ceefax, Oracle. *Interactive videotex* where information is carried from the computer to the receiver by cable, usually telephone lines. Instead of passively receiving information, users can individually interact with the computer, e.g. Prestel.

vignette   (1) A small decoration without a border.   (2) An image that shades off gradually into the background. Vignetted dots are solid at the centre but fade away towards the outer edge. US equivalent: *fade-out half-tone.*

virgule   The stroke /. See **solidus.**

visual   A sketch that shows the rough layout of material. If the visual is finished to a high degree, it is known as a **finished rough** or **presentation visual**. US equivalent: *comprehensive.*

visual display unit   A cathode ray tube on which the output of a computer can be displayed. It can be used in conjunction with a keyboard or light pen as a means of accepting computer input. Also *VDU*.

viz Abbreviation of *videlicet*, a Latin word meaning 'namely', used to specify items or examples.

volume (1) A book that is one of a series. (2) A set of issues of a periodical, especially over one year. (3) The bulk of paper produced by papers of standard thickness.

volume rights See **rights.**

Ww

warranty clauses Clauses in the contract between authors and publishers. A clause states that the work is original and does not infringe any existing copyright agreements. A further clause requires the author to pay to the publisher the legal costs of actions for libel, defamation, obscenity, etc., arising from the book.

watermark A design in paper that is visible when the paper is held up to the light. The mark is made by the raised pattern of the dandy roll of a papermaking machine.

wayzgoose A printer's annual dinner or picnic.

web A continuous roll of paper.

web-fed Of a printing press that prints a continuous roll of paper, not separate sheets. Reeled paper is normally cut and folded on the printing press. Contrast with *sheet-fed*.

web offset Offset lithographic printing—printing in which the image is transferred onto a rubber-covered cylinder and then onto a continuous roll of paper.

weight (1) The weight of paper expressed in grams per square metre, kilograms per 1000 sheets, or (in the USA) pounds per ream (500 sheets). (2) The degree of boldness of a typeface: light, medium, or bold.

wf Abbreviation of *wrong fount*, a mark used in proof correction to show that a character of the wrong typeface or size has been typeset.

white line A line of space between lines of text.

126

whole bound See **full bound.**

wholesaler A person or firm that buys books in large quantities from a publisher and sells them in smaller quantities to booksellers.

widow The last line of a paragraph when it appears at the top of a page.

window (1) A cut-out area in a flat to allow a half-tone negative to be inserted. (2) A feature of some advanced microcomputer systems in which the VDU screen is split into sections, enabling the operation of different sections of the memory to be seen at the same time. Each section on screen is referred to as a window.

wire binding See **mechanical binding.**

wire side The side of the sheet of paper that is in contact with the wire mesh of a papermaking machine. It sometimes shows a light impression (*wiremark*) made by the wire.

wire stitching Binding using wire staples rather than thread. Staples are inserted from the front and clinched at the back.

wood engraving A wooden block cut in relief, made by cutting against the grain.

woodcut A wooden block cut in relief, made by cutting with the grain.

woodfree paper Paper made only from pulp that has been treated chemically, and free of mechanical wood pulp. US equivalent: *free sheet.*

word break The division of a word at the end of a line by using a hyphen.

word count facility Found on some document-based word processing systems, the number of words keyed in at any one time appears on the screen. The facility is useful for people such as authors who write to a specified number of words.

word processing   The electronic storage, editing, and manipulating of text using an electronic keyboard, computer, and printer where text is stored on a magnetic medium except for final output which is in the form of print on paper.

word processor   An electronic device used for the storage, editing, and manipulation of text and consisting of a keyboard, an internal memory or storage, external storage, logic, and printer.

work and turn   The printing of one side of a sheet of paper then, after the sheet is turned over, the second side is printed from the same forme.

wove paper   Paper that shows in its fabric the very faint marks of a fine wire gauze sieve or mould, rather than the pattern of parallel lines of laid paper.

wrap-round   A small group of pages, such as half-tones, folded around a signature so that half precede the signature and the rest follow it.

wrapper   The removable paper cover of a book.

wrong fount   The typesetting of a character in the wrong typeface or size. Also *wf*.

WYSIWYG   Abbreviation of *what you see is what you get*, used to refer to the exact reproduction on a printer of graphics displayed on the screen of a visual display unit.

Xx

x-height   The height of a lower-case x (i.e. a letter without an ascender or descender), used to gauge the height of a particular typeface.

xerographic copier   A plain paper copier which uses an indirect process, i.e. an image of the original is projected on to a drum and charged with an electrostatic charge. Ink powder (toner) is showered on to the charged image. Bond paper is brought into contact with the drum and an electrostatic charge on the pressure roller beneath the paper causes the inked image to transfer from the drum to the paper. It is then exposed to heat which fixes the image. This process only takes a few seconds from start to finish.

Yy

yapp   A soft binding case with overlapping edges.

Zz

zinco   A zinc-coated relief block used in letterpress printing.

Appendix

Proof correction marks

The following proof correction marks are classified in three groups:
Group A: General.
Group B: Deletion, insertion, and substitution.
Group C: Positioning and spacing.

The classified list of marks is an extract from BS 5261: Part 2: 1976 and is reproduced by permission of the British Standards Institution, Linford Wood, Milton Keynes, MK14 6LE.

Classified list of marks (Table 1 from BS 5261 : Part 2)

NOTE: The letters M and P in the notes column indicate marks for marking-up copy and for correcting proofs respectively.

Group A   General

Number	Instruction	Textual mark	Marginal mark	Notes
A1	Correction is concluded	None	/	P Make after each correction
A2	Leave unchanged	– – – – – – under characters to remain	⟨✓⟩	M P
A3	Remove extraneous marks	Encircle marks to be removed	✕	P e.g. film or paper edges visible between lines on bromide or diazo proofs
A3.1	Push down risen spacing material	Encircle blemish	⊥	P
A4	Refer to appropriate authority anything of doubtful accuracy	Encircle word(s) affected	(?)	P

Group B   Deletion, insertion and substitution

B1	Insert in text the matter indicated in the margin	⋀	New matter followed by ⋀	M P Identical to B2
B2	Insert additional matter identified by a letter in a diamond	⋀	⋀ Followed by for example ⟨A⟩	M P The relevant section of the copy should be supplied with the corresponding letter marked on it in a diamond e.g. ⟨A⟩
B3	Delete	/ through character(s) or ├────┤ through words to be deleted	♂	M P
B4	Delete and close up	⌢ ⌡ through character ⌣ or ⌢ ├───┤ ⌣ through character e.g. chara**ȼ**cter chara**ᴄᴛ**cter	♂	M P

133

Number	Instruction	Textual mark	Marginal mark	Notes
B5	Substitute character or substitute part of one or more word(s)	/ through character or ⊢———⊣ through word(s)	New character or new word(s)	M P
B6	Wrong fount. Replace by character(s) of correct fount	Encircle character(s) to be changed	⊗	P
B6.1	Change damaged character(s)	Encircle character(s) to be changed	✕	P This mark is identical to A3
B7	Set in or change to italic	——— under character(s) to be set or changed	⊔	M P Where space does not permit textual marks encircle the affected area instead
B8	Set in or change to capital letters	≡≡≡ under character(s) to be set or changed	≡	
B9	Set in or change to small capital letters	══ under character(s) to be set or changed	══	
B9.1	Set in or change to capital letters for initial letters and small capital letters for the rest of the words	≡≡≡ under initial letters and ══ under rest of word(s)	≡══	
B10	Set in or change to bold type	∿∿∿∿∿ under character(s) to be set or changed	∿	
B11	Set in or change to bold italic type	∿∿∿∿∿ under character(s) to be set or changed	⊔∿	
B12	Change capital letters to lower case letters	Encircle character(s) to be changed	≢	P For use when B5 is inappropriate
B12.1	Change small capital letters to lower case letters	Encircle character(s) to be changed	≠	P For use when B5 is inappropriate

Number	Instruction	Textual mark	Marginal mark	Notes
B13	Change italic to upright type	Encircle character(s) to be changed	⨆	P
B14	Invert type	Encircle character to be inverted	↻	P
B15	Substitute or insert character in 'superior' position	/ through character or ⅄ where required	˥ under character e.g. ²⧸	P
B16	Substitute or insert character in 'inferior' position	/ through character or ⅄ where required	∟ over character e.g. ⧸₂	P
B17	Substitute ligature e.g. ffi for separate letters	├───────┤ through characters affected	⌒ e.g. ﬃ͡	P
B17.1	Substitute separate letters for ligature	├───────┤	Write out separate letters	P
B18	Substitute or insert full stop or decimal point	/ through character or ⅄ where required	(·)	M P
B18.1	Substitute or insert colon	/ through character or ⅄ where required	(:)	M P
B18.2	Substitute or insert semi-colon	/ through character or ⅄ where required	;	M P
B18.3	Substitute or insert comma	/ through character or ⅄ where required	,	M P

Number	Instruction	Textual mark	Marginal mark	Notes
B18.4	Substitute or insert apostrophe	/ through character or ∧ where required	˙⁊	M P
B18.5	Substitute or insert single quotation marks	/ through character or ∧ where required	⸜⁊ and/or ˙⁊	M P
B18.6	Substitute or insert double quotation marks	/ through character or ∧ where required	⸜⸜⁊ and/or ˙˙⁊	M P
B19	Substitute or insert ellipsis	/ through character or ∧ where required	• • •	M P
B20	Substitute or insert leader dots	/ through character or ∧ where required	(• • •)	M P Give the measure of the leader when necessary
B21	Substitute or insert hyphen	/ through character or ∧ where required	⊢−⊣	M P
B22	Substitute or insert rule	/ through character or ∧ where required	⊢⊣	M P Give the size of the rule in the marginal mark e.g. ⊢1em⊣ ⊢4 mm⊣
B23	Substitute or insert oblique	/ through character or ∧ where required	(/)	M P

Group C Positioning and spacing

Number	Instruction	Textual mark	Marginal mark	Notes
C1	Start new paragraph			M P
C2	Run on (no new paragraph)			M P
C3	Transpose characters or words	between characters or words, numbered when necessary		M P
C4	Transpose a number of characters or words	3 2 1	1 2 3	M P To be used when the sequence cannot be clearly indicated by the use of C3. The vertical strokes are made through the characters or words to be transposed and numbered in the correct sequence
C5	Transpose lines			M P
C6	Transpose a number of lines		——— 3 ——— 2 ——— 1	P To be used when the sequence cannot be clearly indicated by C5. Rules extend from the margin into the text with each line to be transplanted numbered in the correct sequence
C7	Centre	enclosing matter to be centred	[ ]	M P
C8	Indent			P Give the amount of the indent in the marginal mark
C9	Cancel indent			P
C10	Set line justified to specified measure	and/or		P Give the exact dimensions when necessary

137

Number	Instruction	Textual mark	Marginal mark	Notes
C11	Set column justified to specified measure			M P Give the exact dimensions when necessary
C12	Move matter specified distance to the right	enclosing matter to be moved to the right		P Give the exact dimensions when necessary
C13	Move matter specified distance to the left	enclosing matter to be moved to the left		P Give the exact dimensions when necessary
C14	Take over character(s), word(s) or line to next line, column or page			P The textual mark surrounds the matter to be taken over and extends into the margin
C15	Take back character(s), word(s), or line to previous line, column or page			P The textual mark surrounds the matter to be taken back and extends into the margin
C16	Raise matter	over matter to be raised under matter to be raised		P Give the exact dimensions when necessary. (Use C28 for insertion of space between lines or paragraph in text)
C17	Lower matter	over matter to be lowered under matter to be lowered		P Give the exact dimensions when necessary. (Use C29 for reduction of space between lines or paragraphs in text)
C18	Move matter to position indicated	Enclose matter to be moved and indicate new position		P Give the exact dimensions when necessary
C19	Correct vertical alignment			P
C20	Correct horizontal alignment	Single line above and below misaligned matter e.g. mis aligned		P The marginal mark is placed level with the head and foot of the relevant line

Number	Instruction	Textual mark	Marginal mark	Notes
C21	Close up. Delete space between characters or words	linking ⌣ characters	⌢	M P
C22	Insert space between characters	| between characters affected	Y	M P Give the size of the space to be inserted when necessary
C23	Insert space between words	Y between words affected	Y	M P Give the size of the space to be inserted when necessary
C24	Reduce space between characters	| between characters affected	⋀	MP Give the amount by which the space is to be reduced when necessary
C25	Reduce space between words	⋀ between words affected	⋀	M P Give amount by which the space is to be reduced when necessary
C26	Make space appear equal between characters or words	| between characters or words affected	Ⅹ	M P
C27	Close up to normal interline spacing	(each side of column linking lines)		MP The textual marks extend into the margin
C28	Insert space between lines or paragraphs	⟶⟨ or ⟩⟶		M P The marginal mark extends between the lines of text. Give the size of the space to be inserted when necessary
C29	Reduce space between lines or paragraphs	⟶⟩ or ⟵		M P The marginal mark extends between the lines of text. Give the amount by which the space is to be reduced when necessary